MANUFACTURING CHANGE

3 Personal Case Studies

Bedford Bruno

April 2018

CONTENTS	PAGE #
INTRODUCTION	2
MY JOURNEY	3
CASE STUDY #1: SIMPSONVILLE, SC 1989 - 1991	6
CASE STUDY #2: MEASHAM, UK 1997-1999	56
CASE STUDY #3: DOVER, DE & MONTREAL, CN 2013-2017	90
OVERALL SUMMARY	128
ACKNOWLEDGEMENTS	129

INTRODUCTION

After over 40 years in the working world, I retired from Edgewell Personal Care at the end of September 2017. My experiences during that time incorporated 4 years in the US Army, working for 12 companies in 15 different locations while living in 20 different houses, working with multiple technologies in diverse industries, and dealing with significant change at every turn. At the suggestion of an old high school friend, I started to write about those experiences beginning with my personal journey. That book led to another and then another, and before you knew it I had 5 books written – most of them short on focused topics. They are all available on Amazon:

1. My American Dream, remembrances of a military brat (my memoirs with picture inserts)
2. Change in Manufacturing – The One Constant, a life's experiences and what I've learned
3. The Organization Lever, a key driver of change
4. Realizing Your Full Potential, and maximizing your contribution to the world
5. Leading Change, style and substance

Of all my professional experiences, 3 stand out as the most significant in terms of scope, complexity and my personal development. This book is about them. They span almost 30 years and represent my progression from a young plant manager to a senior manufacturing leader on the cusp for retirement.

MY JOURNEY

I was born to children of Italian immigrants. All 4 of my grandparents came to the US from Italy through both Ellis Island in NYC and New Orleans. My father was born in NYC and my mother in the rural south of northeastern Arkansas - a farmer's daughter. My father avoided the rackets and mafia through enlistment in the army and fought in World War II in the pacific. He met and married my mother after the war in El Paso, TX. She had left the farming life and was a stewardess for American Airlines at the time. He was an officer and they would make their life in the military. I was raised a military brat which meant moving every couple of years from army post to post. For my sister and me, change was the norm from a very early age. Sports became my way of integrating into every new situation. I played all of them but specialized in basketball. When we moved to a new location, I would find the nearest hoop and court and there would be my new friends. I became extremely competitive and that helped me adapt to any new situation.

After returning from Japan for my final years in high school, I met my future wife. It didn't take me long to realize that she was the one – she was 16 and I was 17 and we've been together ever since. During that time, I had the best athletic experience of my life. Our basketball team would just miss winning the Maryland state championship, but I developed a reputation that would serve me well in college.

I went to the University of Notre Dame on a ROTC scholarship and played varsity basketball for a couple of years. It was a great experience. After moving continuously, I was finally stable living in a community of great young men who had the same values and we would do anything for each other. That bond would last a lifetime. 4 years went quickly, and, in a flash, I was married to my high school sweetheart and a 2nd Lieutenant in the US Army!!

The military experience was great. It was a steep learning curve and extremely fulfilling. I was fortunate to have great mentors and leaders. To this day, I remember them as among the best I've had throughout my life. I was finished my active duty career as a company commander for a combat engineering unit. This is normally a senior captain billet, but I was appointed as a junior 1st Lieutenant based on my performance as a platoon leader and company executive officer. At the young age of 25, I commanded a company of 160 soldiers that were combat qualified and ready to deploy at any moment. It was the culmination of my military career and it couldn't have prepared me better for a lifetime of change and leadership.

My first 8 years out of the military were focused on adjusting to the manufacturing world and learning how to best contribute. I was a degreed mechanical engineer, so the logical start point was in an engineering position leading projects. From there I moved to increasingly more responsible leadership roles in multiple manufacturing sites. My final role during this period was with Frito Lay in Allen Park,

MI as an assistant plant manager leading all technical aspects of the operation – maintenance, engineering, quality and productivity.

The last 30 years I've been leading manufacturing operations of all different types. (nonwoven fabrics, eyeglasses, automotive, specialty chemical, baby wipes, industrial products, Wet One wipes, Diaper Genie, and feminine care products – tampons/pads/liners). The plants ranged in size from small (50 employees) to large (800 employees). I was also responsible for groups of plants on a number of occasions during my career. My challenges included shutdowns, start-ups, consolidations, new product introductions, and union contract negotiations. But in 1989, I had just closed a plant in Greenville, SC and was taking on a much larger challenge with the flagship plant of the Nonwoven Division in Simpsonville, SC. That is where the story begins.

THE SIMPSONVILLE PLANT (1989-1991):
Designing a team-based system to ensure competitive advantage

CHAPTERS

1. Background and situation
2. Entry into the situation
3. THE SHOCK – immediate aftermath and actions
4. THE OPPORTUNITY – to create a sustainable competitive advantage
5. The consultant and initial meetings
6. The process of change, sustainment and renewal
7. Starting to engage in the work – a personal development journey
8. How to impact the cultural shift
9. The VAP (value adding process) and the manufacturing system
10. Creating a Developmental Organization
11. Role development, "uniqueness" and team organization
12. Overall organizational creation and development
13. The results and trajectory – step change and pursuit of perfection
14. Wrap-up
15. Closing comments

1. **BACKGROUND AND SITUATION**

This case study is about the design of a team-based system in Simpsonville, SC. In order to create a competitive advantage for the site in the midst of a tremendous shock to that business, organizational design was selected as the primary lever. Thinking frameworks are used to illustrate the process for the design. First, let's start with some background information.

I joined James River in the late summer of 1987 as Plant Manager of the Greenville resin bonded nonwoven plant. James River (JR) had just purchased the Arkon corporation that was owned by Dexter Hagy, a well-known entrepreneur in the area. Arkon was started in 1972 with the Greenville plant being the original plant with a single carded resin bonded line. A second line was added in 1978 to support the growth of the business which served both the diaper cover stock and the dryer softener sheet markets. The company expanded again with a new plant and 2 more production lines in Simpsonville. It was a modern thermal bonded nonwoven plant primarily serving the diaper cover stock market. That market had moved away from resin bond and towards thermal bond due to the improved softness of the thermal bonded product. The results of that shift were negative for the Greenville plant but very positive for the new plant. The Greenville plant was significantly underutilized when I took over, and the Simpsonville plant was operating 7 days a week, 24 hours a day.

When I started at the Greenville plant, Dexter Hagy and the original Arkon leadership team were being displaced by experienced leaders from within James River and outside the company. That new leadership team had extensive experience with high performance manufacturing systems as the leaders came from Procter and Gamble and Scott Paper Company, both companies were leaders in team based, organizational systems design. My initial mandate at the Greenville plant was to make that business profitable within a year or close the plant and move the remaining business to the Simpsonville plant. Within the year significant operating improvements were made with both material yields and operating efficiencies at a much-improved level. But the technology itself was not capable of delivering the costs needed to make the business viable — at my 1 year mark the decision was made to close the plant. The Greenville plant met its final commitments while transitioning the remaining business to the Simpsonville plant. One of the final accomplishments of the plant was a production record on the last day of operation. We were also able to place all remaining colleagues in jobs in the community. I was fortunate that the plant manager of the Simpsonville plant was leaving the company and I was offered the plant manager position. I was excited. After 2 years of watching the business decline and working to close a plant, I would be taking on the Nonwoven Division's flagship plant and working with that leadership team to take it to the next level.

2. **ENTRY INTO THE SITUATION**

As I was getting used to the new surroundings, some differences with the Greenville plant were evident. The Greenville plant was much smaller at around 50 employees compared to the Simpsonville plant which had around 175. At Greenville we worked hard to build a strong team that was tightly connected to each other. We didn't have much hierarchy — there were the shift teams and then the plant leadership team — basically, your lean and mean approach to running a plant. At our summer picnic, everyone was there, and it was truly a family and team affair. There was a sense of caring in Greenville where Simpsonville was a harsher environment. Simpsonville had 6 levels of hierarchy from shop floor operator to plant manager. (Operator < Team Leader < Shift Supervisor < Day Shift Supervisor < Production Manager < Plant Manager). The plant manager worked through his staff and was much more command and control in approach. The organizational design reflected his style with many different functions and silos. Everyone stayed in their lane, and issues in between lanes could be very political.

Even though the Simpsonville plant was relatively new with modern technology, the operating performance was not what I would expect. Both scrap and efficiency performance were at best average. But the organization had grown to the point where, even running continuously 7 days a week, the business was marginally profitable. The most noticeable anomaly was an hourly to salary ratio of almost 1 to 1. Clearly the overhead burden was too high and a drag on the business. My take-away from the first couple of months on the job were clear — average performance, poor teamwork and an organization that was too big and dysfunctional. I knew what had to be done and was ready to get to work when the unimaginable happened!

3. **THE "SHOCK" — immediate aftermath and actions**

In 1985 JR acquired all of Crown Zellerbach's pulp and paper operations which included 2 nonwoven operations. These were combined with their other operations and the 2 Arkon plants to form the Nonwoven Division, which would report under the Towel and Tissue business unit. This new structure created Research & Development and Engineering functions at the division level charged with developing and pursuing new technologies and applications for nonwovens fabrics. As a part of this initiative, JR entered into a number of joint ventures – one involving a South Korean diaper manufacturer. This activity would have a significant impact on the Nonwovens Division and the Simpsonville plant.

Three months after entering my new role as Plant Manager for the Simpsonville plant we lost our largest customer – Procter and Gamble. They had decided to move their business elsewhere as a competitive response to James River's increasing threat to some of their core businesses – one of which was the JV described above. This meant a 40% reduction in production volume for the plant and turned a marginally profitable 7-day operation into a significant loss and the need to lay-off a large number of people. After coming from a plant closure situation in Greenville, the folks at the Simpsonville plant were beginning to think that I was a jinx. There was no time to worry about that, we had to respond and do it quickly.

With production going from a 7-day operation to around 4 days, the first order of business was to get the direct staffing right – what would be the best shift configuration to meet the current business need and make it scalable as business increased in the future? At a 7-day operation, we were running 4 12-hour crews. We decided to go to 3 8-hour shift scenario. This enabled us to eliminate all overtime, keep our skills at a stable level, and be in a better position to ramp-up as we picked up volume in the future. It was always in the back of our mind that we would go back to a 7-day continuous operation as additional business was secured. Our job now was to build the best foundation to enable that to happen.

After the direct staffing level was set at 3 8-hour shifts, we now had to build the rest of the organization to support it. We had to do it in a very aggressive way to ensure we took out all the costs necessary to maintain our competitiveness, and it had to be scalable as we increased our volume over time. I saw this as an opportunity to get flatter and eliminate the silos that caused many of the communications issues. I led a small design team of plant senior leaders in this process. Due to the sensitivity of the topic, I chose a closed process for this to do it quickly, knowing that we would need to make adjustments. I did the design work myself and got feedback from the design team, and then we went with it. We reduced the # of levels and functions – for instance, we had a senior manager for maintenance, one for projects, one for quality, one for productivity – in the new design there was just one manager. We were fortunate to have some high-quality leaders in the plant that could take on multi-functional responsibility. For the indirect hourly employees, we looked at the necessary work and the shifts of operation and decided on the right staffing. We did this, again, with an eye to the future of getting back to 7 days operation.

My experience with the Greenville plant told me that speed of action was important in order to get the change behind us and be able to move forward in the best way. Once the folks at Greenville had a clear view of the future, it was much easier to focus on the day to day operations. I took all of the actions outlined above in the first few weeks and communicated broadly throughout the plant and to other key stakeholders. I wanted everyone to know that we were done with making the adjustment and now needed to focus on creating a new future. Simultaneously, I was working with Sales and Marketing to ensure that they had all hands-on deck to get us back to our optimum operating scenario – which for a nonwoven plant was a 6 to 7-day operation a week. I never let up on the pressure of our commercial group to get the business back. At the plant, we would do whatever was necessary to support them. I always had them in the plant giving updates to the folks, so they never forgot about us.

With such a massive change, I knew that my knowledge could only take us so far. My boss had experienced changes more in line with what we were facing at Simpsonville, so he recommended a couple of consultants that he had used in the past. His guidance to me was – get some help, you need to take this opportunity to make Simpsonville the most competitive plant that it can be! I never forgot his advice. From that point forward, my focus was two-fold – 1/ Maintain the current stability of operations and improve it; and 2/ Create the best organization for the future to enable optimal production at Simpsonville.

4. **THE OPPORTUNITY – To create a sustainable competitive advantage**

I was fortunate to have experienced operational leaders as my senior managers. They provided excellent guidance to me and were available at any time. My immediate manager was the VP of Operations for the Nonwoven Division. He had led the start-up of a new plant with Scott Paper Company and was a clear and concise communicator. He knew the importance of organizational design in order to optimize the overall performance of a site, but he also knew that there were many different processes that you could use. When he gave me 2 consultant names to contact, he said that their processes were very different and that I would have to choose with the plant leadership team the best fit. We knew that our costs were too high which made the margins unacceptably low. Operating performance was a part of the problem, but the size of our organization was way out of whack compared to our production requirements. Our targets were to be world class in terms of operating performance – material yields and efficiencies. We generally knew where we needed to be – scrap under 5% and OEE over 85%. With just 2 production lines, a focused effort would get us there in a year to two time-frame.

Organization size was not as clear. We knew it had to be much less than current, but where should we settle out? The only way to understand this was through a formal organizational design process. This is where the help of the consultant would be critical. But I had to be the primary leader working hand in hand with the consultant and providing the necessary leadership in the plant to drive the needed change. During this time James Rivers significantly reduced the capital available to the Nonwoven Division due to their expansion efforts in Europe. This raised the level of importance in creating a high-performance organization in Simpsonville as a way of maintaining competitiveness. I was excited about the process and the potential to make significant strides and be able to realize the full potential of the plant and its people.

5. **THE CONSULTANT AND INITIAL MEETINGS**

The two consultants that we considered to help us were very different. Both had excellent resumes and worked with leading companies, but we needed to determine the best fit. The first consultant came to visit the plant and laid out their process from start to finish. It was more of a cookie cutter approach but covered all the bases and we could easily see where we were headed and how we would get there. My leadership team really liked the consultants and their approach – it was easy to follow and made a lot of sense. The 2nd consultant came in with a very general process and a number of frameworks to guide our thinking relative to possible directions. He provided no answers just different processes to help us think through the various issues. At the core, his belief was that the leadership team and the plant had to be fully engaged in the process and be the designers of their future. His role was one of guide and mentor. If not, the change would not be sustainable and when the next shock hit the plant and business, the capability would not exist to push through and ensure the viability of the plant and business.

Intuitively I was attracted to the second consultant. Ken Wessel was raised a farm boy and dealt with all of the challenges of a family farm – scarce resources with timely requirements that needed to be met. There was always low hierarchy and he and his family always figured out the most effective way to get the work done. He majored in Industrial Engineering at the university and accepted a job with Procter and Gamble in a manufacturing plant as an Industrial Engineer. He learned quickly that using the stopwatch was not the way and there were other, more important things to consider in order to optimize the plant performance. Ken ended up the operations manager of the most successful high-performance work system design start-up at their soap factory in Lima, OH. He went on the lead the conversion of P&G's oldest union factory to a team-based design after that. He was now a full-time consultant helping a range of clients just like us. Needless to say, I convinced the staff that Ken was our guy and I hired him quickly after our initial meeting. One of the first frameworks that Ken shared with our leadership team was one of Personal Development.

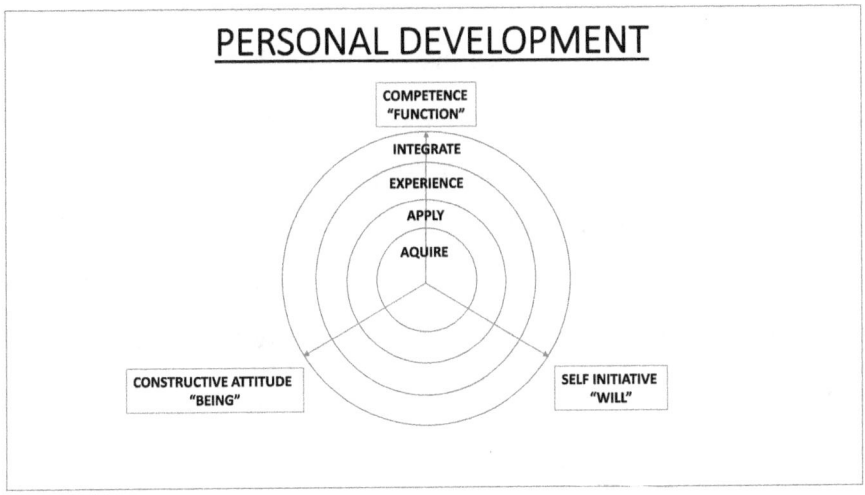

This framework illustrates the necessary components of the Personal Development process relative to any subject. It also defines the pathway to fully integrate the subject into our own capabilities. As an illustration, it is our role as the Simpsonville plant leadership team to design the new organization. In order for us to do this we have to acquire the knowledge relative to the design process, apply it to the realities of the current plant situation, experience the design impact as we progress, and finally ensure the final design is fully integrated into our own leadership process on an ongoing basis. In this process we have to grow on the axis of 1/ Competence relative to organization design; 2/ Develop a constructive attitude to ensure best interactions with others; and 3/ Always take the initiative to move things forward and proactively engage in the process. This set the stage for the leadership team to fully engage in the process. Only by doing so can the process be cascaded through the plant and the final organization design be deployed effectively.

Ken shared other frameworks with the leadership team early on to provide a glimpse of the work that we would embark on. We used these frameworks to start to understand our external environment and to further the development of our leadership team. As we developed and learned more, Ken would share other frameworks. Eventually, we began to see the overall system that he was using to guide us. This was the essence of his developmental approach – as we were ready, he would take the next step.

6. THE PROCESS OF CHANGE, SUSTAINMENT AND RENEWAL

One of the initial steps in setting the direction for any entity is to understand the expectations for it from the environment. In the case of the Simpsonville plant it was important to understand the expectations from James River as a company and the Nonwoven Division as a business. In the ideal case everyone at the plant would understand the direction of both the company and business, and how the plant and they and their teams fit into the picture. In essence it was all about what was required of them and why was it required. The framework below outlines a process to help an organization and people think through this.

STRATEGIC THINKING FRAMEWORK
(output aims to work through and create)

Essential Activities	Roles or Functions			
	Leading Thrust towards a desired achievement, and order while carrying it out.	**Planning** A motivating relationship between reality and objectives that describe a new reality.	**Managing** Effective allocation and use of resources toward the achievement of objectives.	
Strategic Define the business we're in and what it takes to succeed in its markets.	1: PERFORMANCE	3: CORPORATE DIRECTION	5: PURSUITS	S
	2: CAPACITY	4: PORTFOLIO DIFFERENTIATION	6: PREMISES	P
Leadership Evoke and channel efforts to maximize effectiveness of VAPs.	13: CREATE STAKEHOLDERS	15: STRATEGIZING INTEGRATION	17: INTENT	S
	14: OPPORTUNITIES	16: COMPETITIVE DYNAMICS	18: COMPETITIVE STRATEGIES	P
Operational Do work in ways that meet standards and continually improve processes and products.	9: SPIRIT & WILLFULNESS	7: ISSUES	11: PROJECTS	S
	10: MATERIALIZATION	8: TANGIBLE FACTORS	12: SYSTEMS	P

The matrix organizes the activities in such a way that enables an individual or group of individuals to think through the process from the strategic to the operational level. Within each level there are leading, planning and managing functions to consider. Within each of the functions at each level there is a structure of activity and patterns that help to fully define that area. For example, at the strategic level in the leading function the structure component is the performance necessary to be successful and in order to deliver that performance on a consistent basis a pattern of capacities must be present within the organization. The numbers in each box provide the order that you would process the framework to best facilitate a discussion. Always start with the strategic level, then go to the operational level with issues first, and then to the leadership level. The logic is that the requirements set forth at the strategic level will always create issues at the operational that need to be worked through to be successful. The leadership level deals with how to connect the two levels through the best utilization of the organization. There are definitions for each box that help to better understand the detail to be developed, but for purposes of this case study we will talk in more general terms.

The way we processed this at Simpsonville was to have a small group discussion with the key leaders in the company and business. We used the framework to guide the discussion. The intent was to fully understand the strategic requirements and what issues surfaced at the plant level that had to be addressed and managed. After the small group discussion with the key external stakeholders, we asked some of them to come to the plant and give a presentation to the leadership team that summarized our discussion and provided direction for us as we developed the Simpsonville direction and plans. This became a standard process for us and the framework was a key tool that we used on a continuous basis to help guide us through the process. Some of the key takeaways for us from this process were not surprising and some were eye opening. For example, we knew our cost were too high and that the plant was underutilized, but we didn't fully understand what the margin expectation was and how large of a gap we had. It was also clear that the plant leadership team and the people in the plant were not very knowledgeable relative to the company and business direction, nor did they fully understand what was expected of them and why? The process itself was insightful and helped ground us all on what we needed to deliver to the company and business to ensure our long-term viability.

The activities of the leadership level are all about the most effective use of the organization to ensure the operational is hard wired to the strategic. The description of that level is intended to characterize its importance; "To evoke and channel efforts to maximize the effectiveness of the plant's value adding processes". This level answers the questions; 1/ How do we create key stakeholders in the plant? 2/ What are the opportunities we have to focus them? 3/ How do we ensure that our strategies are fully integrated within the plant? 4/ What are the competing strategies for our resources and what are the priorities? 5/ What is the overall intent and direction for our operation? And 6/ How does our pattern of competitive strategies align with that intent?

The output of this process led to the development of the Simpsonville plan – we called it the Simpsonville Architecture to describe a process of construction and building. The framework is outlined below:

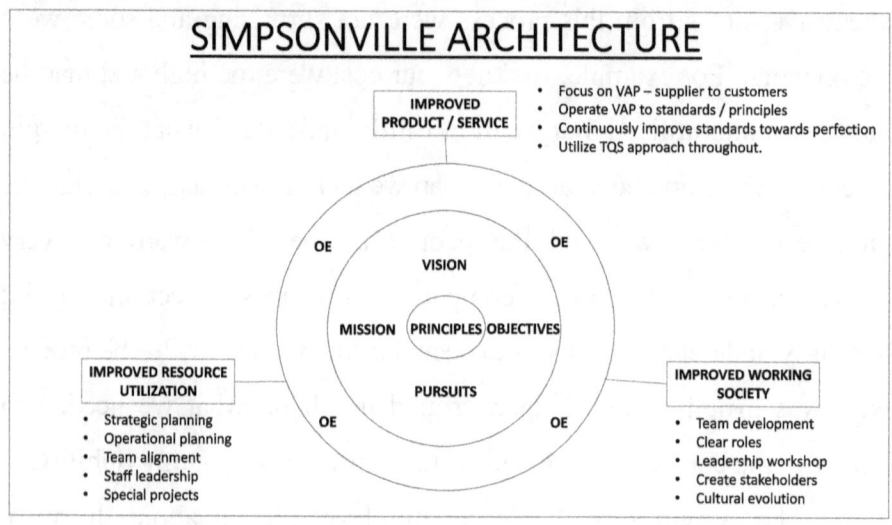

Our Simpsonville Architecture incorporated key operational and leadership activities from the strategic framework and was linked to the company and business strategic direction. With all of this input we developed the plant strategic direction. We called in our VMOP (Vision, Mission, Objective and Principles) – they were directly in support of the company and business' higher-level pursuits. The layer of OE (Organizational Effectiveness) depicts the use of our system of frameworks to translate that direction throughout the organization. We were focused on 3 major areas of improvement: the quality of our products and service to our customers, the quality of our working environment and the development of our colleagues, and the effectiveness of our overall resource utilization processes. Once our VMOP was developed, we knew the areas of activity to develop further and the OE methodologies helped us frame them in the most effective way. This framework provided a guide for us as we progressed through time. The VMOP provided the direction but we continuously renewed it to ensure any changes to the external environment were immediately incorporated into our process. We realized the importance of translating all of this to the actual work that was being done on a daily basis on the shop floor. The following framework helped us organize that work in the most effective way:

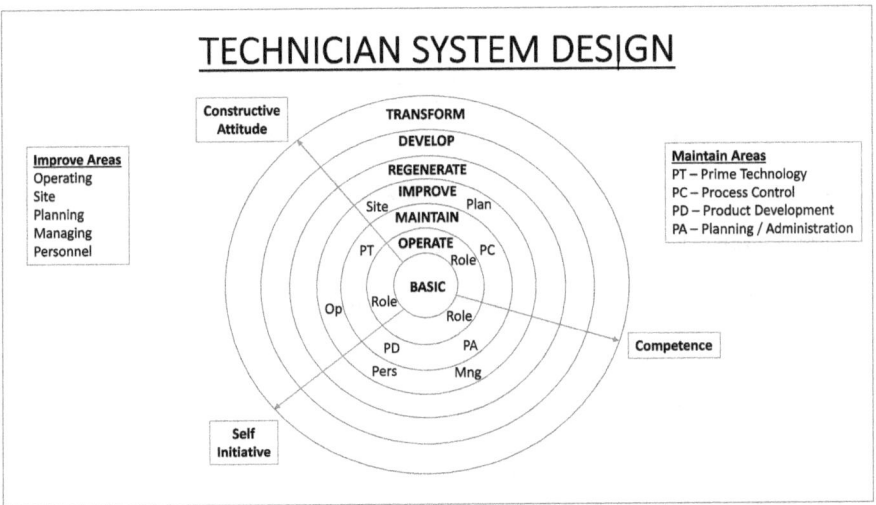

The Technician System was our hourly pay and progression system. The framework depicts how the system worked but there was much more detailed information involved in the actual execution of the system. It shows the progression of an entry level operator as they develop their capability in support of the plant and business needs. The progression is as follows:

- Basic is entry level – new colleagues learn a job to perform in support of the Operate level colleague and work on their progression to get to that level. To be fully qualified at the Basic level a new colleague must be qualified to perform one operating role.
- To be fully qualified at the Operate level a colleague must be qualified to perform multiple roles – the number is determined based on the area of the plant.
- To be fully qualified at the Maintain level an operator must have the capability to specialize in a certain area along with continuing to perform their normal operate level roles.
- To be fully qualified at the Improve level an operator must have the capability to lead a significant plant wide change and demonstrate success based on results achieved.
- The Regenerate, Develop and Transform are higher level qualifications that are developed based on special needs at the plant or business – these are determined by the plant leadership team.

The qualification at a certain level has 4 gates:

1/ The colleague must demonstrate that they can do the job to certain performance standards over an extended period of time. (competence)

2/ The colleague completes an improvement project related to the area of qualification. (competence)

3/ The colleague goes through a peer review to gain feedback on their team functioning capability (i.e. constructive attitude and self-initiative).

4/ The team that the colleague is a part of must have met their objectives for the month. (If team objectives are not met all qualifications are carried over to the next month)

The qualification process is intentionally focused on individual competence, constructive attitude and self-initiative; and overall team performance. As colleagues become more qualified they must maintain their capability in all the areas. Part of the team process is to schedule the work so that their members are able to maintain their qualifications and new qualifications can be supported. The expectation is that all hourly colleagues must be qualified through the Maintain Level in 2 years. This provides broad capability throughout the plant that can continuously be deployed against current operating requirements and needed improvement areas.

In order to support the continuous development of the plant colleagues, we put in place a learning center with computer stations that was manned on a 24-hour 7-day basis. Colleagues were provided time each week to support their development, but they also could do work on their time. The primary driver of qualification were business needs and the self-initiative of the colleagues. We set the wage rates at a higher level to reflect the value add that the company was gaining from colleagues moving from level to level. There was separate progression for maintenance hourly to reflect a different type of curriculum and need.

In summary, the Technician System was critical to the evolution of the Simpsonville plant for the following reasons:

- It put in place a system for continuous development in direct support of the plant Value Adding Processes.
- It was driven by business need and the self-initiative of all colleagues.
- It set an expectation of continuous development by everyone, every day.
- It was hard wired to meeting objectives and improvements.
- It placed managers and other salaried colleagues as enablers and supporters of the process.
- It focused on realizing the full potential of everyone in the plant and was a fully integrated system.

7. STARTING TO ENGAGE IN THE WORK – A PERSONAL DEVELOPMENT JOURNEY

At the beginning Ken Wessel met with me and my leadership team periodically as we worked through the process from the strategic level to the operational. Simultaneously, we were working with the realities of the situation and adjusting our staffing and organization to reflect the new production requirements. The organization would continue to develop and evolve as we gained a better understanding of how to fully utilize our colleagues. 2 frameworks that we continually used to help guide us were the one on personal development and the activity tetrad. Both were designed to guide process development and help us in charting our courses. The next framework is a variation on one that I've already shared.

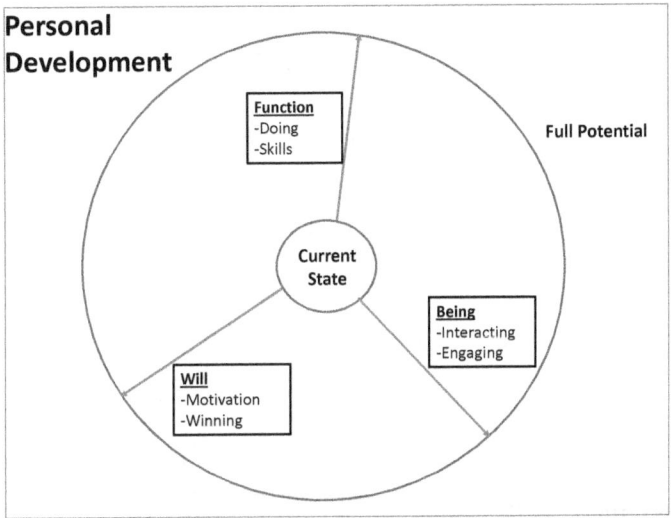

In every area that we were working, we always designed the process to ensure: 1/ We were learning the subject matter in the most effective way; 2/ The learning process was interactive and involved engagement with others to share different perspectives; and 3/ That we were developing our will at the same time – the drive to use our new capability to make a difference in the operation. It was all about realizing our full potential and support that development in others. This process was engrained in everyone and in everything that we did.

The Activity Tetrad was a simple framework that enabled us to think through "the doing" of anything.

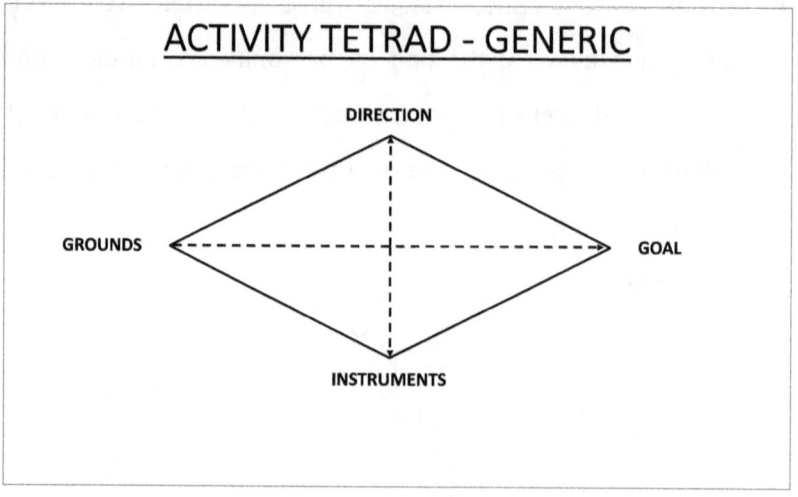

In doing anything, you had to have a clear understanding of your "Goals" – you have to know where it is that you are going!! You had to know the "Grounds" that you were on – that's in relation to the goal. Once these 2 points were known, you had to think about the different ways to get there and decide on the best "Direction" to use! Once direction is set, the development of a number of "Instruments" to help guide you along the way is important to keep you on track. The Activity

Tetrad is a simple but powerful way of thinking and guiding you in doing anything. In the remaining pages of this case we will look at some of the organizational design considerations. They include:

- Managing the cultural transition towards the desired state.
- Managing personal evolution in support of the cultural transition – Function, Being and Will.
- Understanding the Core Value Added Process (VAP) analysis and developing a site environmental map.
- Creating a Developmental Organization.
- Creating and developing powerful roles within the context of Developmental Organizations.
- Structuring teams in support of role development.
- The formal organizational design process.
- The organizational picture – designing from the VAP out.

8. **HOW TO IMPACT CULTURAL SHIFT**

The Activity Tetrad is useful in a discussion on impacting a cultural shift. It's an activity that is critical to the success of the creation of a Developmental Organization. Spending time with the leadership team on the topic is very useful in establishing a pathway for the shift and how to manage it. The framework below uses the thinking of the generic framework but tailors it for our purposes.

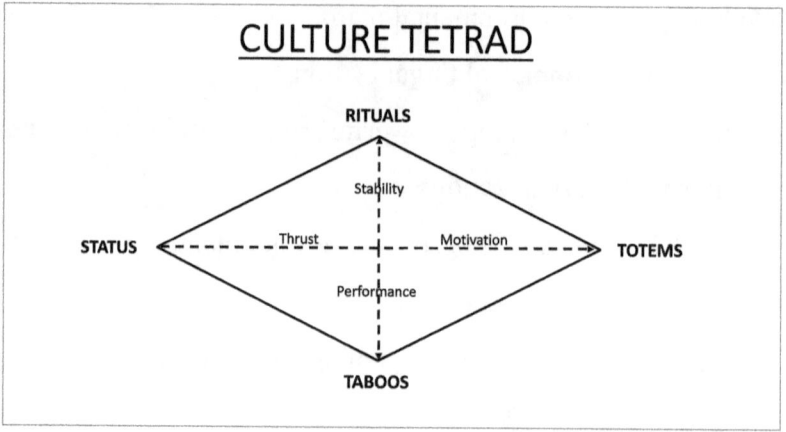

The Ground for the Culture Tetrad is "Status" or what values do we want to give status to? The Goal for the tetrad is "Totems" or what signs or banners represent the values that have high status? The "Rituals" provide the routines or direction that enable you to demonstrate the Totems. The "Taboos" represent things that we don't want represented in our Culture. An example of the Culture Tetrad as it's developed for one value or status area would be for Personal Development:

31

- Status or Value – Personal Development.
- Totems:
    - Learning Center open 24 hours a day, 7 days a week.
    - Fully integrated plant level personal development process.
    - Expectation of Self Initiative as a key driver of the process.
    - The Technician System – Pay linked to development and contribution.
- Rituals:
    - 360-degree peer feedback review process.
    - Quarterly development review process for everyone.
    - Qualification celebration process for Technicians.
- Taboos
    - Blaming people for making mistakes.
    - Not having time to support the development of a fellow colleague.

We used the culture tetrad to develop our thinking relative to other values that we felt were critical in the development of our culture such as: teamwork, self-initiative, supporting others, continuous improvement, customer orientation and safety. The result of our discussions were multiple totems and rituals that were represented throughout our organization. They served the purpose of keeping our core values top of mind for everyone in the organization. Another framework that shows the representation of culture in another context is up next.

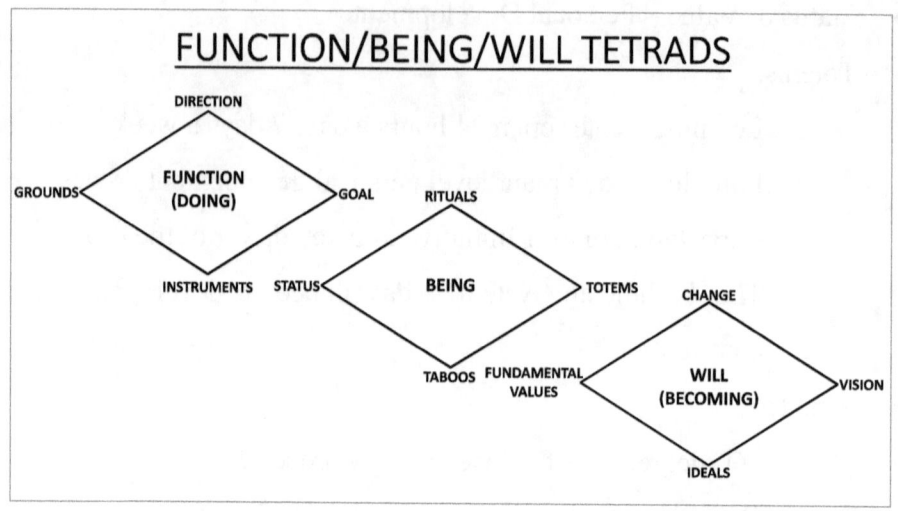

Again, the framework is intended to help us think through a process either individually or within a group. In terms of our personal development, we grow along 3 dimensions – Function, Being and Will. Function is our competence or knowledge in doing things; Being represents how we do things in alignment with the organization core values; and Will is our motivation to improve and be better every day. The 3 tetrads represent that activity. We discussed Being as Culture earlier. The Function tetrad is along the lines of the Generic of "Doing". The Will tetrad enables us to better understand how to improve it. Again, it's grounded on the fundamental values relating to our culture. We have to think through what that Vision is for us. Then as we are thinking about our Current State, we need to identify how to change in line with the Vision and, finally, define an Ideal to use as an instrument to measure progress.

This is the power of the OE technology and the use of frameworks. It helps us think through important issues either individually or as a team. The results of that process are changes that moves us along in the direction that we need to go.

9. THE VALUE ADDING PROCESS AND THE MANUFACTURING SYSTEM

The focus in a manufacturing environment must be on the value adding process (or the material flow). For the Simpsonville plant the fiber comes in from suppliers and is converted step by step to packaged roll goods that go to customers. P&G was one of the customers – they use nonwoven roll goods in the manufacturer of baby diapers. The challenge for any manufacturing organization is to focus all energy and effort in operating and improving those processes. Simpsonville's overhead had grown so large that there was a lot of wasted effort and many distractions that took away from the most important activities. The foundation of building a high-performance organization is understanding the fundamentals of the value adding processes and constructing the optimal organization. Let's look at some frameworks that help in the understanding of our core process requirements.

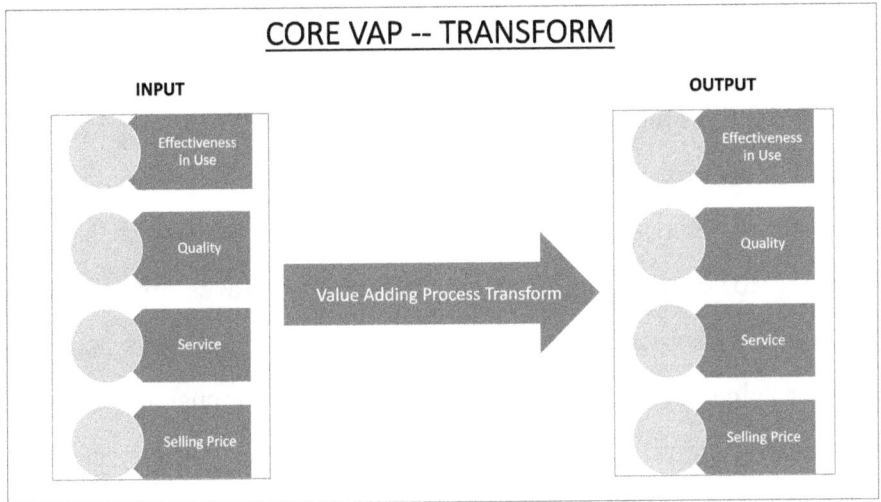

Each value-added process is made up of a number of steps or transforms. For the Simpsonville Plant, starting with the supplied fiber, they are: fiber blending < fiber opening < carding < calendaring < winding < slitting < packaging < warehouse < shipping. At each step and within each transform value is added in some way. That value is represented in terms of the customer's needs in 4 different areas:

- Effectiveness in Use – for diaper cover stock that had to do with fluid flow from the baby to the absorbent core or "how effective is our cover stock?"
- Quality – this has to do with the consistency of the product relative to the specification necessary to meet the customer's needs or "what is our process capability?"
- Service – this has to do with the delivery of the product on time as ordered by the customer or "what are our lead times?"

- Selling Price – this has to do with the cost to produce the product to the margin requirements of the business at the selling price agreed to with the customer or "what is our cost of goods?"

At each transform value is added in these areas. The manufacturing challenge is always to operate the value adding process to a set of standards to ensure the proper transformation takes place and to continuously improve those processes over time. It is always helpful to view our value adding process through the eyes of our customers. In any audit or shop floor "Gemba" walk (a Lean term), we always start from the customers perspective and walk back through the process and check the performance to the output requirements. That process is reflected in the next framework.

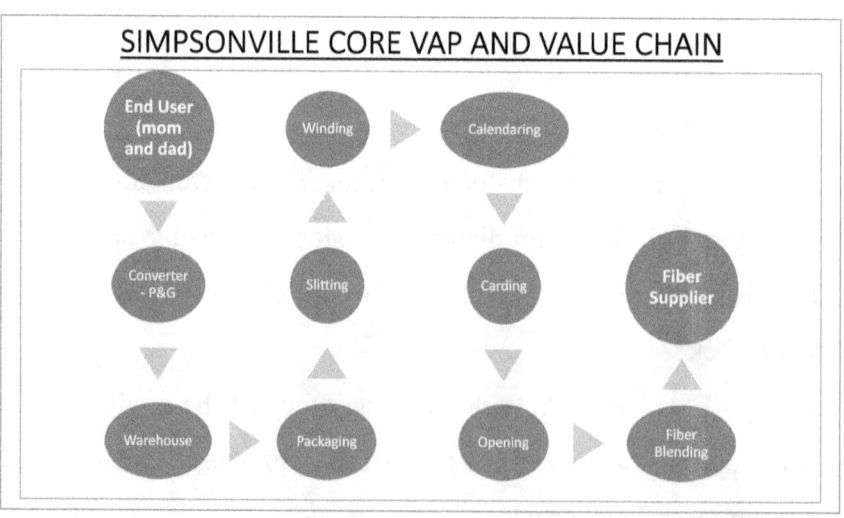

The entire organization should be focused on operating and improving the value adding processes. In this world management, leadership and resources are always out on the shop floor observing the situation, understanding the problems and improving the operations. Any effort not related to this is wasted and must be eliminated. In the Lean world, the focus is on relentlessly driving waste out of the system. There is always work to be done in organizations that is not directly related to the value adding processes, but it's important that we understand why we do the work and how it fits in our system, and not just do things because we've always done them. Let's take a look at Simpsonville's Environmental Map to get a perspective on what that additional work may be.

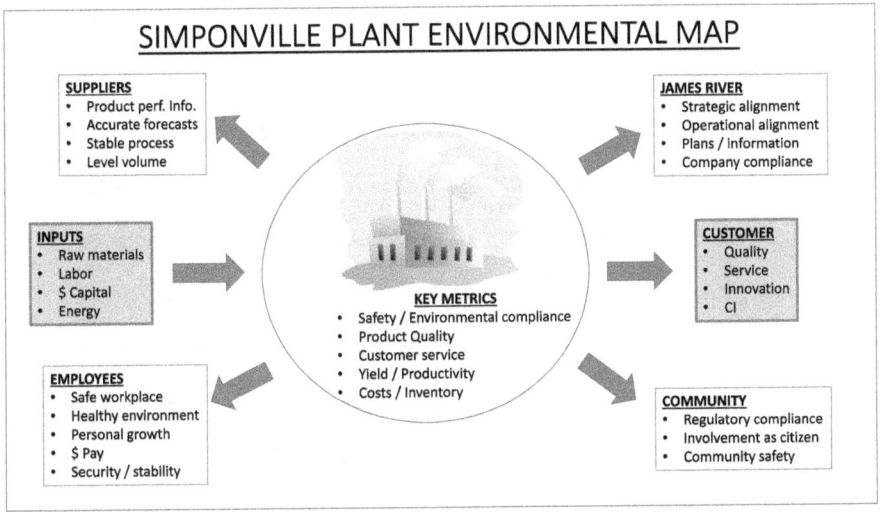

The Inputs > Key Metrics > Customer axis has to do with the value adding processes. The other boxes have to do with other key stakeholders that have needs that must be met and managed. It's important that the leadership team purposefully assess those stakeholders and needs to define the activities that must be managed. This effort is critical but must be managed in a way that keeps the focus on what's most important which is the value adding process.

The analysis described in this chapter is fundamental in defining the work of the organization. It is the start point in the creation of the organization structure, systems and process that will carry out that work. But before we move on, I want to add an overview of value adding processes that was provided by Ken Wessel during our work (these are his words using the terms of the tetrad).

"Every purposeful, viable organization creates products and/or services that are judged by its stakeholders to be essential in meeting their needs, and that provide overall value beyond what they could find elsewhere. Their response includes providing their supplier with value in return such that both parties and their relationship is sustained. This may be referred to as a value chain, linked by core purposes.

Delivery and support of products and relationships is made possible through the action of a sequence of value adding processes that acquire material inputs of a specified value (from a supplier/source) and transform them to output products of higher value as specified by stakeholders. This may be referred to as a core process, which is the source of vitality and is the life force in each stakeholder in a value chain.

Excellence in management of the value adding process (VAP) then becomes a critical success factor in the health, growth, and life of any organization and a matter of concern to all value chain stakeholders. The following premises describe what is required to achieve the desired level of excellence:

- *Ground for management of the VAP is based on purpose of providing direction to and enhancing the natural behavior of materials through achieving exactness in the action of assets on materials, achieved through skillful control of asset performance by individuals who are able to manage themselves as the ultimate source of VAP management.*
- *The goal of managing a VAP includes being a fully dependable source of value as specified by stakeholders, and the freedom to operate independent of them in developing own vitality and viability.*
- *Direction in managing a VAP is maintained through a system of feedback and adjustment loops that:*
  - *Continuously compare input/output value with what is specified.*
  - *Measure, evaluate, and upgrade the exchange of value between the organization and its stakeholders.*
  - *Promote strong, unbuffered linkage between performance of individuals and value to stakeholders.*
  - *Identify and respond to emerging needs and opportunities.*

- *The primary instrument for managing the VAP is an individual who is able to exert constructive influence over it. This capability includes:*
    - *Complete knowledge of what perfection is in the transforming of materials.*
    - *A mental picture of forces that cause materials to change at each step in the VAP.*
    - *Experience in dealing with source and effects of variance to the ideal.*
    - *Systemic grasp of interaction of skill, actions, asset performance and material.*
    - *Effective management of own actions, state, and purposes.*
    - *The evolution of quality of thinking as key element in management of self.*

Value adding process mapping is a valuable technique in developing capability to manage the VAP:

- *VAP mapping is a business-based process that depicts the essential transitions, transaction, and transformations that take place as materials are acted on by assets toward the ultimate goal of fulfilling stakeholder needs.*
- *A VAP map identifies the centerline/core of materials movement in the context of its surrounding business environment. It defines the nature of work required to manage it in order to sustain and extend the life of the surrounding business.*

- *The mapping process is increased in value by bringing together a variety of sources with differing views of the VAP: i.e. operator, business leader, customer, engineer, R&D technician.*
- *Mapping points out and leads to the integration of the vital natures of energy: physical, emotional, and mental; required for excellence in VAP management."*

10. **THE DEVELOPMENTAL ORGANIZATION**

We can use the Activity Tetrad to represent a Developmental Organization. At the Simpsonville plant, we set as our organizational intent to develop such an organization. Through Ken Wessel's resourcing we felt that such an organization would realize the full potential of the plant and create a sustainable competitive advantage for the plant and business. The framework below describes its essence.

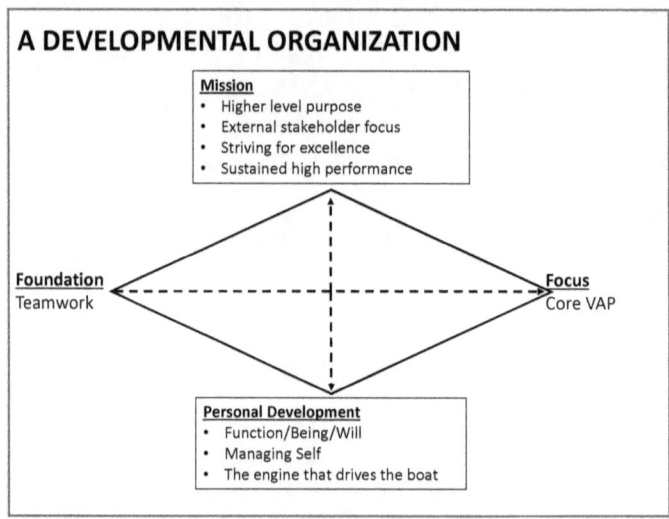

The foundation of a Developmental Organization is teamwork. The teamwork is always focused on operating the core value adding processes to a set of standards while striving for excellence. The Direction is set based on the defined Mission which supports customers and key stakeholders at a high level of performance. The primary instrument is the personal development of everyone in the organization — every day and in every way!! The development is defined along the 3 dimensions of function, being and will; with a strong emphasis on managing one's self in the best interests of the team and organization. The tetrad, as it's laid out, defines the primary levers to focus on in order to move towards this type of organization. Many of the things already discussed are involved in bringing such an organization into existence. It doesn't happen overnight — at Simpsonville it took a couple of years just to get onto the right track.

11. **ROLE DEVELOPMENT, "UNIQUENESS" AND TEAM ORGANIZATION**

To facilitate personal development for all colleagues, an understanding of roles and how to define them more holistically is important. At a high level we want everyone to have a powerful role and significantly impact the operation. We may have to start smaller, but always with the expectation of continually building capability in support of increasing contribution. As people develop themselves over time, the organization gets stronger and the operating performance gets better. The next framework outlines a holistic view of role development.

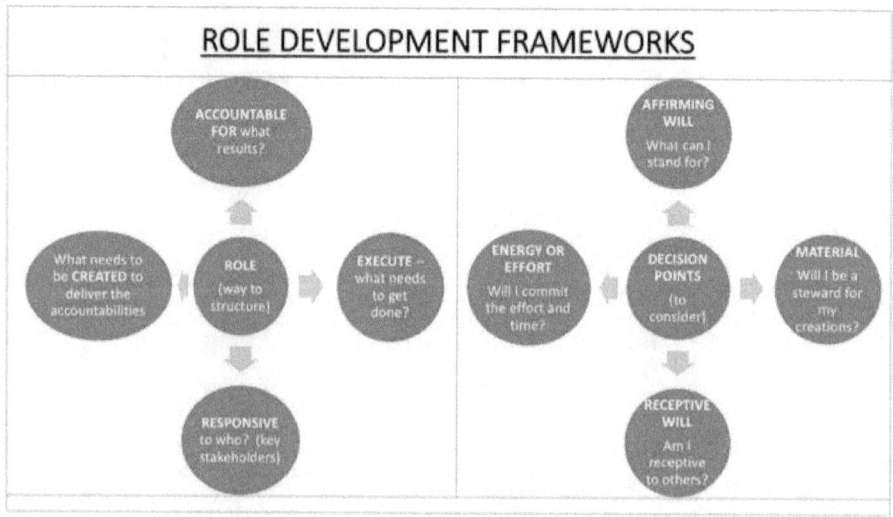

The left side of the framework defines a role and the right side shows the considerations needed in accepting the role. The role always starts with a "reason for being" — and that is it's accountable for delivering certain results — they must be defined clearly. In delivering the needed results there are key stakeholders for the role that have expectations that must be met. This defines the "What". Next up is the "How" and the plan of execution of the role. In order to execute flawlessly, certain capabilities must be learned and in place. In a Developmental Organization all roles are thought through in this manner. In accepting a role and committing yourself 100% to it, you must think through other things such as: What can I stand for? Am I (Will I be) receptive to others? Am I willing to commit the necessary time and effort? Will I be a steward for my creations in this role? To be successful in a role, it must be flushed out thoroughly per the framework, but you also must Affirm that you are willing to do whatever it takes to be successful in the role. If everyone has done their work relative to role development, the organization is well on its way towards high performance! Another framework can be helpful in understanding the performance requirement in a role or a team.

```
┌─────────────────────────────────────────────────────────────────┐
│            STAR FRAMEWORK – STATE OR NATURE OF BEHAVIOR         │
│                                                                 │
│                            Uniqueness                           │
│                       What's special about us?                  │
│                        (individuals or teams)                   │
│                                                                 │
│        Lower Limit                            Upper Limit       │
│  • The very least needed to      • The extent we could aspire to.│
│    express uniqueness   RANGE  our  POTENTIAL                   │
│  • Minimum acceptable standard  CUSTOMER  • The most we could   │
│                         Or who we are       imaging doing.      │
│                           Serving       • What can we conceive of?│
│                        (even markets)                           │
│                                                                 │
│         Nourishment                            Mastery          │
│  • In development of state, what   • Things in us we exert more │
│    do we provide for environment     mastery over (can't say no)│
│    to nourish it?                  • What must we do to deliver │
│  • Tapping back to be able to        that uniqueness?           │
│    provide energy.                 • MASTER – In our environment│
│  • What do we need to be             we are controlled – i.e.   │
│    nourished?                        can't dictate to the customer│
└─────────────────────────────────────────────────────────────────┘
```

In this framework, we are trying to understand the range of performance that is acceptable in a role or within a team. We also want to push the limits on what might be possible. The intent is to insure the minimum expectation is always delivered and drive towards our aspirations. Always pushing the boundaries is a key aspect of Developmental Organizations. It's not just hoping but understanding what we need to master to reach our aspirations. Also, where we get our nourishment is critical, this gives us the material and energy to keep pushing. A doctor pushing the boundaries of Melanoma Cancer research always get their nourishment from the patients and their families and the lives that they are improving! Thinking through these two frameworks will enable you to understand and organize yourself to deliver to expectations and push the limits that will result in significant and continuous personal development. Once the initial role development work is done, the teams need to look at their collective work and make sure that everything is covered. The following framework facilitates the discussion.

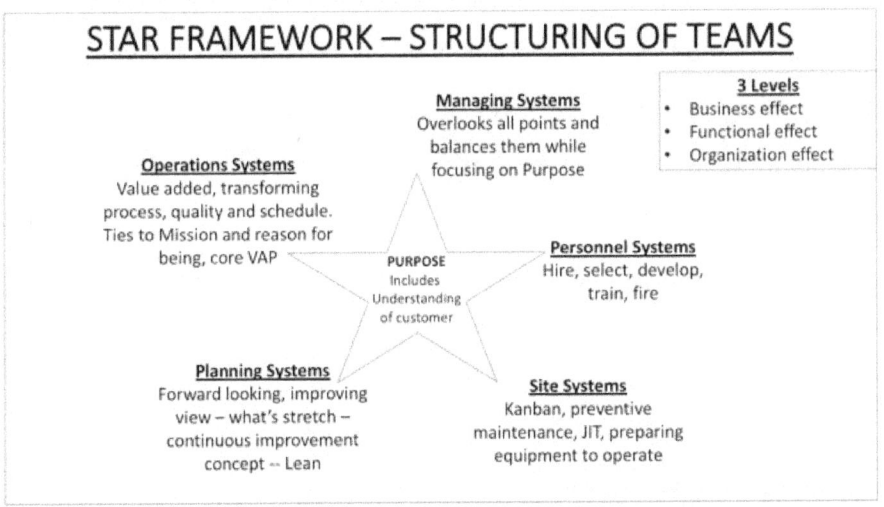

All teams have a purpose and serve customers, but this must be defined in a succinct manner. Once this is understood that activity is defined, and roles are developed. But there are always other things to be managed within a team setting beyond the doing of the work. This framework organizes and structures teams around a star model — the doing of the work is represented by the Operations point. In order for the operations to be able to do the work the working site must be prepared and ready to go — this work is represented by the Site Point. In order for the Operations to execute the activity, they must have the right number of trained and capable people — this work is represented by the

Personnel point. In order to ensure the Operation meets the requirements of stakeholders and customers, requirements must be understood, materials ordered, and production schedules developed — this work is represented by the Planning Point. All the coordinating and managing activity is represented by the Managing Point. Using this framework can be helpful to the team to ensure its work is viewed in a holistic fashion and organized accordingly. Now that we've looked at role and team development, let's see how we build an organization from there.

12. **ORGANIZATION CREATION AND DEVELOPMENT**

Organizations are normally not designed and just evolve over time. Maybe in the beginning there was a determination of the number of operators needed and then a traditional top down organizational chart developed to understand all the jobs and then standard job descriptions developed. If we consider how we develop new products, there is a totally different process as we design them to fulfill certain functions and purposes. We want to get the design just right in order to optimize the performance of the product. Why would it be any different for organizations? There are many consultants and processes out there that can take you down this path. Our process was pretty clear based on all of the discussion that we've had so far. We were grounded in the Developmental Organization concept and were going to focus the organizational design on the operation of the value adding processes while striving for excellence. The next framework outlines the process.

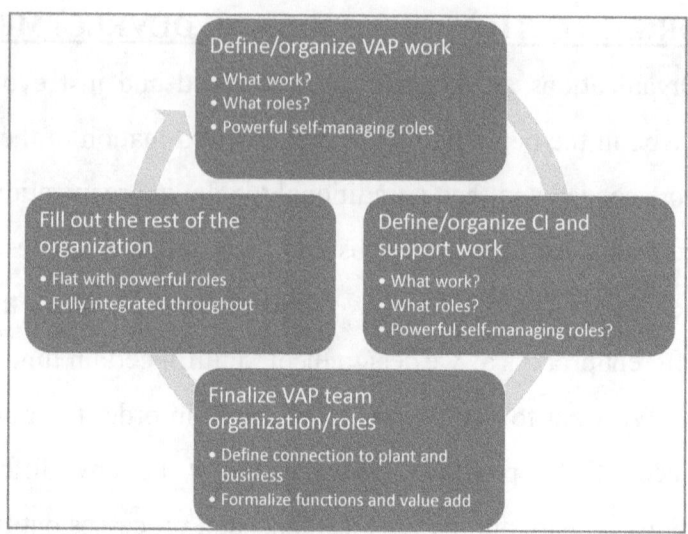

We are building the organization from the value adding process out, always with the intent to create powerful roles for our colleagues to fill, grow into and realize their full potential – all to the organization, plants and business benefit. Once we've framed the VAP related roles, we have to connect them with the other critical connecting work – this is where the STAR framework can be helpful in identifying that work and developing strong roles for it. We always want to guard against taking focus away from the value adding processes and ensure activity and organization don't become burdensome. This is always the challenge -- higher levels always want things done. It is the job of local leadership to determine the value-added work and push back when needed. If we take a look at the value-added process level, our organizational design can be represented by the following framework. Compared to the original organization of 6 levels, the Self Managing Work Team organization has

3 levels to the Plant Manager level — it is a VAP out organization rather than a top down one.

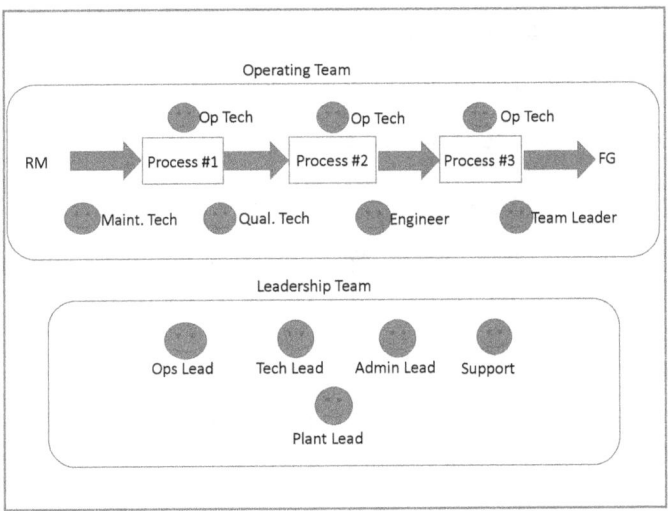

The design must follow a process and be well thought out, but it is always in development. As people grow and develop at different rates, the organization changes form to take advantage of their expanding capability. As learning takes place on the best combinations for roles, changes in role configuration will occur. Remember, organizations are made up of people, and as such are always adapting to circumstances, growth and learning. Traditional organizations rarely change and in doing so, waste much of the capability of its people – they stagnate and its reflected in the results that they achieve over time. Improvement in results and achieving excellence is all a function of the growth and development of people and the effective utilization of their capabilities!

13. THE RESULTS AND TRAJECTORY – STEP CHANGE AND PURSUIT OF PERFECTION

The improvement in results over the 2-year period after the impact of the 40% loss in production volume was significant. A snapshot of that improvement would include:

- 60% waste reduction from 13% to 5%.
- 10% uptime (efficiency) improvement from 82% to 90%.
- Over $2 million savings in fixed cost based on reduction of organization size from 175 to 125 colleagues (this was after the production volume was back to 7-day level)
- 15% reduction in COGS (cost of goods sold) driven by $4 million in savings.

More importantly, the capability was built into the organization to drive continuous improvement and a pursuit of excellence. The Technician System development was at the core of this engine. It meant that the hourly colleagues were driving their development and improvement every day and the rest of the organization was providing the proactive support necessary to move forward. This change helped to ensure the long-term viability of the site. Since my time as leader of the site, newer technologies have emerged that have put pressure on the site and its products, but the organization continues to maintain its competitiveness. I haven't been back to the plant since 1995, although I stay in contact with some of the players who are still in the area – maybe I'll make a trip back in the near future!

14. **WRAP-UP**

As I reflect on my key learnings from this period, certain things come immediately to mind:
- It's always about people and their relentless pursuit of excellence and teamwork.
- Anything of lasting value takes thought, hard work and strong leadership from the top.
- In times of crisis we have a mandate to do extraordinary things – do we really need a crisis??
- It does take certain types of people to thrive in this environment – selfless, driven and caring.

My experience at the Simpsonville plant set the tone for every leadership role that I have taken since. I was very fortunate to have had this opportunity early in my manufacturing leadership career as it provided the foundation to approach every new challenge that I've come across since. Thinking back now, I wish I could go back in time and observe the process as it was unfolding. I'm sure there would be many more learnings that I didn't pick up on at the time.

15. **CLOSING COMMENTS**

The Simpsonville situation challenged me to go deeper into my experiences to find the capability that enabled me to provide the right leadership. I was fortunate to have a mentor in that journey. It would be the start of a long friendship and partnership that I would have with Ken Wessel. He and I would work together many times in the future – it just seemed like he brought out the best in me. I think back on the leadership team at Simpsonville and what a great group we had. They accepted my leadership and enabled me to do what I had to do and grow tremendously. I've moved many times since those days and have lost track of most of the key folks, but the memory of our work during that period remains fresh in my mind.

As I thought about doing this case study, I was looking through some of my old books and material and stumbled upon a notebook. The notebook had the memos and notes of many of the meetings and processes that we had developed. As I went through the notebook it brought back many of the memories and names of all the key players. I was also able to recreate some material that was not there that I remembered to be critical to the process. That notebook and my memory are the basis for this book.

The 2nd case starts 6 years after I left my Simpsonville plant manager role. In the interim I had experienced a significant amount of change.

THE MEASHAM PLANT (1997-1999):
A new automotive plant start-up in the UK

CHAPTERS

1. Background and situation
2. The Anderson plant – key learnings
3. First exposure – interviewing for the new job
4. Arrival – adjusting personally and professionally
5. Starting at the Telford plant
6. Moving to Measham and running our own show
7. Growing pains – need more space
8. Start-up and relationships with the automotive plants
9. My departure – the plant continues to improve
10. Learnings applied to Saltillo
11. The results and trajectory – step change and pursuit of perfection
12. Wrap-up
13. Closing comments

1. **BACKGROUND AND SITUATION**

This case study is about the start-up of a new automotive tier 1 parts supplier plant in the UK. I was the 2nd person hired for that plant, and in 2 years we were producing bumpers for 3 major automotive customers with 350 people in the plant. To better understand the context of this situation, it's important to review some of my earlier experiences and the buildup to that job.

After 8 years of stability in Greenville, SC; I was in the midst of significant change both personally and professionally. I left Fiberweb in late 1995 to take on the plant manager role of a large sunglass making facility (Ray Ban) for Bausch and Lomb near Deep Creek Lake in beautiful Western Maryland. It seemed to be a dream job as it was one of the leading facilities of its type in the world. Three months after arrival, I was called up to Rochester, NY and told the plant would be closing in 1 year and the business would move to Nueva Laredo, MX! This was quite a shock for me as we had just bought a home on the lake, and, with the announcement of the closure, the housing market collapsed. Bausch and Lomb (B&L) was the largest employer in the county, and the community could not easily absorb the loss of that many good paying jobs.

Fortunately, when I received my offer from B&L I had another from Plastic Omnium that I was considering. Plastic Omnium was a French, privately held company with annual sales of around $1 billion. I had a great interview with them and got along well with their President in the US. I called him up and told him of my situation. He said that they had not filled the job yet, and could I meet his boss from Paris at the Atlanta airport to see if I might be acceptable a second time around? I said OK, we met, and they extended the same offer a second time. I was off to Anderson, SC to try my hand at the automotive world!

Since it was early in 1996 and with the family settled and the kids in school, I went off to the new job while the family remained in Deep Creek. It was always a key principle for us to maintain stability for the family unit as much as we could. We had 3 kids now in elementary and middle school, and my wife and I always tried to minimize the disruption. She and I were both military brats and moved continuously as children. In the military environment there was always strong support systems, but not so in the civilian world. I was on my own starting a new job while the family enjoyed the lake and wrapped up the school year.

2. **THE ANDERSON PLANT – KEY LEARNINGS**

When I arrived at the Anderson plant in South Carolina, the situation was dire. My first week I was in meetings with both customers, one in each conference room, to work through supply expectations and issues. We were behind our start-up learning curve and were struggling to keep up with the ramp-up of the customer's assembly lines. It became clear to me that there was nothing that I could do, and we had to meet their requirement or be fined large sums of money. My position and most of the plant leadership team should have been in place fully a year earlier, so we were playing catch-up in a big way. We had a French start-up team that was doing most of the heavy lifting but the knowledge transfer to the local folks was not going well – there were language and cultural issues that I could see immediately.

The President and I agreed that we had to get ahead of the curve as quickly as possible, and that money had to be spent now. We built the organization quickly knowing that we had far too many people for a "steady state" operation and were able to stay just ahead of our customer's ramp-up expectation. As is normal in the automotive world, painting is always the challenge and the bottleneck. It's a science and an art, and the standards are very high on the quality requirements. It took us awhile to get ahead in the paint shop, but we were fortunate to get a team from England to come help us out. If not for them, we would have failed – they got us over the hump and we were able to stabilize and become more efficient. We went from crisis to stability and were on the improvement curve within my first year. Fortunately for me, I had almost 6 months on my own and was able to focus all my energy and effort on the situation.

I received my Ph. D. a little over a year prior to taking the PO job. My dissertation was centered around the cross-cultural experience. Little did I know that I would be working for a French company and experiencing the shock that happens when different values collide. I had read about the differences between cultures and knew what they were between the French and the US. But reading and knowing intellectually; and experiencing are 2 different things. When we were in crisis within my first month of joining the company, I was in a meeting with my boss's boss (the global VP from Paris) when all of sudden he was yelling at me – or it seemed to me that's what was happening! That was one of the many experiences that helped me learn how to navigate the cultural differences in the most effective way – it would serve me well in the future.

Plastic Omnium was one of the most innovative companies in the automotive plastic parts business in the world. The founder, Pierre Burelle, was ahead of his time and foresaw the use of plastic for the automotive industry during and after the World War II. He was still very active in the business that his son now led (Jean Burelle). They both came to visit the Anderson plant in my first year. It was a great visit and you could see that they knew what leadership was all about. They made a habit a visiting all plants globally once a year. During their visit I noticed something. It seemed like there were 2 tours that happened during the visit – the formal one that my team and I planned and executed; and the other one – all the side conversations that the owners had with the French guys in French. I became very sensitive to this process. All of the plants in the world had a contingent of French working in them. These were normally process or product or financial experts. I think both of our tours were consistent, but I would ensure that in the future we had just one culture at the plant and that we all spoke the "same language"!

During the crisis stage in Anderson and, as we moved to stability, we spent a lot of money. Late in my first year, PO sold half the plant (the bumper part) to another automotive supplier (Becker) to get more financial support for the US business. With that move, Becker wanted their own man in the plant manager role as PO had a French president in the US. That meant that my job would go to a Becker guy. Fortunately, I was thought of highly enough by PO to be offered other opportunities. The start-up of a new bumper plant in the UK was one of them. I would take away some key learnings from the Anderson situation:

- Get ahead of the power curve early – front end load the process organizationally to ensure you deliver the customer ramp-up.
- Build one culture at the plant and allow the different country cultures to easily settle in and work with each other.
- Make sure you have the molding and painting experts identified and, in the plant, early and in sufficient number – especially paint!

- Design the roles of the technicians more holistically – use the Simpsonville model to ensure they have maximum impact on the operation and business.

3. **FIRST EXPOSURE – INTERVIEWING FOR THE JOB**

PO was good to their word and made available for me a number of opportunities. They were growing rapidly around the world with plans for new plants being developed in South Africa and the UK. I was open to either opportunity and viewed them as continued personal growth. After conversations with my wife, we decided that the UK one would probably be best – so I was off to interview there.

I had never been to the UK in my travels. I had spent a good deal of time on the continent of Europe, but never made it to the island. My interview was made up of discussions with the senior leadership of PO's UK business and a preview of the plans for the new plant. I felt a reluctance to entertain my candidacy by the local leadership. It was a new culture for me, so it was hard to get a good read on the situation. From my perspective, both personally and professionally, and relative to the family; I felt it would be a great situation for us. I was excited as I headed back home but felt uneasy about their receptivity to me.

In retrospect I realize that it was a very difficult time for the UK and their relationship with PO in Paris. One of my mentors was the VP of Global Operations in Paris (he was the guy who yelled at me!). My leadership in Anderson had been greatly appreciated by him and the French President in the US. They both felt that I had a lot to offer to the UK business, and that I would be open and receptive to their leadership and input. The relationship with the PO Managing Director and his team in the UK was a little strained at the time. I felt like they would prefer to have their own man in the position rather than bring in someone from out of country.

I waited it out in South Carolina and then got the word that I was selected for the position. I was excited, but it meant another change for the family – the 4th since we left the stability of Greenville, SC less than 2 years earlier. We started to make arrangements for the move.

4. ARRIVAL – ADJUSTING PERSONALLY AND PROFESSIONALLY

I arrived at Heathrow with my 2 big bags that had everything that I would need until the final move of the family. Again, the stability of the family was number one priority, so they would wait until school ended and enjoy the summer on the lake (we had bought another lake house in South Carolina). It would be almost 6 months until the family made it to the UK. This would allow me to focus on the job at hand, but I would miss my foundation – that was life! PO had arranged a car for me from Heathrow to the UK headquarters in Telford. I met there briefly with my boss and the HR leader and was off to get settled. They had made accommodations for me to include a car and local bed and breakfast. I put my stuff in the car and got in to drive when I realized it was not only on the other side, but it was a stick shift! Wow, quite a challenge, but I figured it out! I headed off to get settled. Everything in the UK was smaller and compact – the roads, the houses, the refrigerators! I knew it was going to be an adjustment. My bed and breakfast was in Ironbridge about 30 minutes away. It was known as the area where the industrial revolution had started and was an important part of UK history.

After spending the day getting settled, I was at work the next day. The first order of business was getting to know all the key players and to get the lay of the land for the project. The work on the project would start at the Telford plant where they had arranged for a team room for the project team to use until the new plant was ready for occupancy. The new plant had been acquired and had 2 large injection machines that had been used to make trash cans. The plant would be expanded to almost twice its original size, the injection machines would be refitted to mold bumpers and a paint shop would be added. The production start was a year away and the customers were Rover (Land Rover and a new car model) and Jaguar (the new S type). My 2 best buddies were now a French guy and an English gent. I was the second person hired for the plant, the first was David Scrivens who was a project engineer assigned from the Telford plant that would move with the project to Measham. The French guy was Herve Montloin who was the assigned program manager from Paris for this start-up. Looking back now, I realize how fortunate I was to have both Dave and Herve – they were the yin and the yang of the project. Dave represented the needed order and planning of the project, where Herve was creative and aggressive. Herve was also well respected within PO and at the Paris headquarters. Our strong relationship from the start would serve us well in the years to come.

Although I was involved in all aspects of the project planning, my main focus was the organizational side and recruiting. My main role in the project was facilitating a smooth relationship between the UK and the French sides. Although we were on the same team, the different thought processes caused a lot of friction. The French were quick and jumped from topic to topic, while the British were methodical and wanted to fully process subjects and ideas before proceeding to the next. I knew this from my Anderson experience and had gained a good deal of knowledge on the best way to facilitate them in the context of a project. Due to Herve and Dave's leadership the project proceeded according to plan. One battle that Herve had early on with our VP in Paris was the scope of the paint shop. After Anderson's issues, there was a hesitancy to go with full robotic painting in Measham. Herve stood by his guns believing that full robotic was the only way!! He would stay close to the recruiting of the paint technical personal to ensure that we delivered and didn't make him look bad! Although based in Paris, he remained an integral part of the Measham team throughout the duration of the project.

My focus turned to organization and recruiting. My partner in this early on was the HR Director of PO in the UK Caroline Lawler. She was extremely sharp and a great collaborator. She had arranged for all of my personal arrangements and was a bit of a lifeline for me in the early days. I handled the organization design and she was the recruiting lead until we were able to hire our Measham local HR Manager. Our priorities for recruiting were the key plant leadership team and technology experts. They included: HR Manager, Operations Manager, Quality Manager, Logistics Manager, Assembly Manager, Jaguar Program Manager, Rover Program Manager, Paint Expert and Paint Shop Manager, Molding Expert and Molding Shop Manager. While Caroline handled the normal recruiting process, I focused on the technology experts. I interviewed a number of knowledgeable folks to try to identify people who had proven expertise. I would get names, make calls, get other names and continue until I had a number of good candidates.

The outcome of this process was that we got 3 of the best technology leaders that we could have hoped for. In the area of painting, 2 names kept coming up – Laurent Coulon and Nick Jasko. In conversations with others in Telford, Nick's name was thrown out there as one of the best they have had, but he moved on and was no longer in the area. Laurent was known to be the best that PO had. My old boss in Anderson said that I had to get him and, if I did, the painting would be smooth! I set out to get them both – and got them. For Nick, I went to his house about an hour south of the new plant and literally talked him into joining! (He wanted to come anyway.) For Laurent, I was lucky, my French colleagues helped me out and he wanted to come to the UK anyway. In molding, we got Chris Evans who was experienced in automotive molding and just a great guy and perfect fit. Wow, was I lucky there! At the time I didn't know it but securing those 3 guys increased the probability of success at Measham immensely!

The rest of the senior team started to fall into place – what a team – to this day, the best that I have had the pleasure to worked with:

- Plant Director – Buff Bruno (American)
- Engineering/Project Manager – Dave Scrivens (English)
- HR Manager – Bernadette Westmoreland (Northern Ireland)
- Operations Manager – Phil Brown (Scottish)
- Assembly Manager – Jim Harlow (Scottish)

- Quality Manager – Brian Phelan (Southern Ireland)
- Logistic Manager – David Barlow (English)
- Jaguar Factory Project Manager – Simon Palmer (English)
- Rover Factory Project Manager – Richard Wormsley (English)
- Manufacturing Excellence – Steve Grainger (Welsh)
- Injection/Molding Leader – Chris Evans (English)
- Paint Program Manager – Nick Jasko (English)
- Paintshop Manager – Laurent Coulon (French)
- Finance Manager – Sylvain Rousseau – (French)
- Plant Administrative Assistant – Tonya Perry (English)

5. **STARTING AT THE TELFORD PLANT**

Dave and I started the project in the team room at the Telford plant -- no offices, just phones on conference tables. The Measham team grew from there. As people arrived, they took their place at a conference table and took on their respective role. The culture that we were striving for started right there, no silos or boundaries with everyone out for the best of the project and the plant. As the automotive programs kicked in and we started to get requirements for bumpers, we developed a flow and system. While we were at Telford, the Telford plant would injection mold the bumpers and paint them to the specification of the customer and the new Measham team would assemble the bumpers and put them on shuttle truck for delivery to the customers. Telford was an experienced plant and had the capability to make the painted bumper, and we needed the expertise in assembling the bumpers and interfacing with the customer.

It seemed to be a fairly straight forward process, but the rigorous specification of the new customers and the difference in cultures between us and the Telford plant created some issues. The specification required a painting finish that was relatively free of inclusions (paint defects). We were not very integrated into Telford's production process and the feedback that we were providing wasn't accepted easily. Steve Grainger remembers the following exchange "Each morning the Telford paint shop lead would come into our assembly area and see the pile of scrap bumpers and asked why they were there. Brian (our quality manager) and I would say — it's YOUR scrap!!"

We caused a lot of the problem ourselves as we were learning the assembly process. Any touching of the bumper during assembly was an opportunity to create a defect. The key was to design a flow that gave you the rate that you needed with minimum movement and effort from the assembly team. I remember watching our assembly process at the beginning – it looked haphazard and hectic, really not in control. In the early stages we had our managers assembling the bumpers as we were short of people. I worked some shifts and I wasn't very good!! But once we got it down, it was a thing to behold. I remember thinking how easy it looked – did we really get that many bumpers in an hour?!! Phil Brown, Steve Grainger and Jim Harlow were brilliant working with the engineers and the folks on improvements and it really became an art. I got a real appreciation for the Scots and Welsh – they had the total package!

By the time the Measham plant was ready for our move, we were ready to leave Telford. The difference in culture was really wearing on all of us. Things seem to be so difficult as everyone was out for their team and function. We knew we wanted to create a different type of culture and extend how we were operating in Telford to Measham – how do you transfer it and scale it by over 20 times? We were going to find out.

6. **MOVING TO MEASHAM AND RUNNING OUR OWN SHOW**

The move to Measham was planned over a weekend so that we would be up and running by Monday morning. We had a plan with all activities defined and roles developed. We had a strong team and there was no doubt in my mind that we would be successful. The night before the move some of the leaders met at the pub for a "few pints"! For me, even a few is a lot of beer! I wasn't there, but I'm told that they had a lot more than "a few" and it became a national competition between the Scots, English and Irish. The Scots won, and our Irish Quality Manager Brian didn't make it in time for the start of the move! It was a minor issue but one that would become part of the folk lore of the Measham plant.

The move went well, and we were up and running as planned with Telford making the painted bumpers, shipping them to Measham and we assembled them and delivered them to the respective automotive plants. The Measham plant was site selected to be in good proximity to the 3 production lines of the respective automotive programs. We were now in our own plant and building its capability to do all of the production.

During the early period at Measham, politics had escalated relative to Telford and Measham and the status of the overall program. I don't even remember now what the specific issues were, but it was clear that a showdown was coming. A meeting was planned at Measham with all of the top leaders of PO and the Measham senior leadership team. Our

VP of Global Operation from Paris (my mentor), the Managing Director (MD) for the UK, and my boss the Director of Operations for the UK were all at the meeting. Emotions were running high and I remember an argument between myself and the MD of the UK. The VP from Paris tried to calm things down and get us to work together, but I was sure that I would be headed back to the states. It just wasn't a good situation – with my whole team there, I had not provided very good leadership and felt very bad. Before he left to go back to Paris, the VP encouraged me to spend more time with the MD and go the extra yard. One of the guys on my team, Simon, had been with me in Anderson. He led the rescue effort by the UK painters. He knew I took a big hit, and said to me "Buff, remember the UK is not like the US, what is most important is what is not being said – you must figure things out!!" To this day I remember his advice and am thankful for it. I immediately committed more time on my schedule to sit down with the MD and other members of the UK leadership team to ensure I was flushing out all the issues and that I with my team were addressing them. It was another lesson in cross cultural interactions.

7. **GROWING PAINS – NEED MORE SPACE**

As we took possession of the plant and did more detailed process flow diagrams and layouts, it became clear that we needed more space. The initial layout didn't leave enough room for people to operate and interact with one another. Dave and his engineering team created an optimal layout that we wanted to pursue, but it required an expansion to the shipping wing of the plant and more money. I had developed a much better relationship with the MD and he bought on to the change immediately but knew that I would have to sell it to the VP in Paris. Dave and I were off to Paris. This is where having the French connection is critical. Herve commanded a lot of respect in Paris and he was there with us to provide support. We pitched the expansion over a Parisian lunch with wine and got the approval to go forward. Once the expansion was wrapping up, we would be getting ready for the ramp-up with our customers.

As the injection machines were refitted and the paint shop was becoming operational, we were adding our key technical team. Having Chris Evans, Nick Jasko and Laurent Coulon on board early was a blessing. They personally made sure that when the equipment was ready to operate, the people were trained and capable. As we were nearing the start-up, we went through a "mass" hiring process where over a weekend we did interviews with large groups of people to fill out the remaining roles in the plant. Bernadette, our HR Manager, organized the affair and it was structured in a way that our culture continued to build and deepen.

I had created a document early on that outlined the Vision, Mission, Objectives and Principles of the Measham plant. It also spoke to the values that we held and were trying to reinforce. This document was processed repeatedly with the leadership team and became our manifesto. It was the basis for the interview process that Bernadette had created. It was just a wonderful experience and we hired some great folks. The plant was located in the middle of the old coal mining industry which was in tremendous decline. People were happy to have a job and were energized with the culture that we were trying to create.

We utilized the St. Romain plant in France for the training of our paint technicians. Painting was the critical process in our plant, and we wanted them to have actual production experience in one of the best PO plants. Steve Grainger led the contingent and was their "single parent" for the duration of the training. It was a 1-month tour of duty where Steve did everything from coordinating shifts to managing the social calendar of the group. It was a critical process for us — and Steve was the guy to make it happen.

Plastic Omnium was a truly entrepreneurial company and organization. There was an expectation of no waste and a very strong cost consciousness. When we got the money for the expansion, we knew that was it and we had to ensure we could get the project done and not over spend. This forced us to look at flow from every perspective – material, product, people and to optimize office space. Besides developing an optimal process and product flow, we outlined the flow of people from the time they came to work, their breaks, their lunch and when it was time to go home. We created 2 major open office areas – one was the central one and another production one. The central one had all of the project specific and leadership resources, while the production one had anyone who was providing direct support to the operations. Both offices had glass windows and oversaw the plant operation. There were offices from the original plant in the front that were taken up by the HR / Administrative team. Everything was designed to support the work and the optimal flow through the plant.

As the project work was coming to a close, I had a real feeling of satisfaction. The leadership team and organization that we had built was first class, and now that I had a better process interfacing with the MD and his team it seemed like we were hitting on all cylinders. I knew that meeting the requirements for the production ramp-up would be challenging, but I felt the team was ready. With a just in time production system that was linked to the automotive assembly line requirements, there was no margin for error. We had developed a FMEA (Failure Modes and Effects Analysis) and put in place contingency actions in case of high probability failures. We didn't have the budget to create major redundant systems, but we were ready to start operation. I was looking forward to the next phase!

8. **START-UP AND THE RELATIONSHIPS WITH THE AUTOMOTIVE PLANTS**

Our customers at the start-up of the plant were Jaguar, Rover and Land Rover. For Jaguar and Rover, these were introductory models --- the Jaguar X200 S type and the Rover R75. BMW had bought Rover, and this would be their first entry into the car market – there was an expectation of BMW level quality. The Land Rover program would be in support of an upgraded model. We would support 3 different assembly plants that were in close proximity to our plant location in Measham. In the automotive business, 1st tier suppliers (or which we were one) were expected to locate their plants to be able to supply the assembly lines JIT. What this meant is that there was limited storage available in the assembly plants for your product. In the case of our bumpers, we had a truckload or so of fully assembled bumpers staged near our assembly point on the line. We would get the signal on the bumper type and order on the assembly line the day before, so we would assemble on day shift what went on the car in the evening shift. The automotive guys normally operated 2 10-hour shifts a day, 5 days a week. This gave them time for maintenance between shifts and the weekends to handle volume surges. If you had a problem and caused the assembly line to stop, the automotive companies could charge you $3000 a minute that they were down – this covered their fixed cost base. Given this cost, it was an expectation of every 1st tier supplier to have some contingency plan or safety stock.

Our way of handling this was to have our safety stock in painted bumpers. Most of our risk and technical complexity was in molding and painting, so having our safety stock after those processes made the most sense. We also had contingency plans and some redundancy built into our processes based on the high probability/risk areas identified in our FMEA analysis. Our connection to the automotive assembly lines was through our assembly area. Our technicians were always in the customer's plants assessing their issues and the impact to us. If another supplier was having a problem and was going to impact the assembly line, we would know early on and be able to make adjustments to our process. Initially our customers had a problem talking to our technicians. They were used to dealing with managers and salaried people, not hourly workers! But once they realized that our technicians knew more about our and their product than anyone else and had the authority to make decisions, they accepted them and valued their input.

At our plant in Measham we had 6 parking spaces – 2 for each customer. They were welcome in our plant at any time, and we made it clear that we would proactively address any issue or concern that they had. There were no secrets and we treated them as an extension of our team. The primary visitors were the supplier quality folks. Our quality system was QS9000 which incorporated the uniqueness required of each automotive company. Our approach to quality was that each technician was responsible for all aspects of their production to include the quality. They would do the measuring and testing and make any adjustments needed to ensure the right level of quality was in the product. The quality function at the plant was more of a systems audit and continuous improvement one. Quality control was in the realm of operations, while quality assurance and improvement were in the professional quality team.

In the Simpsonville case, I led formal organization design processes as we transitioned from traditional to more team-based processes. At Measham, the design process happened naturally prior to start-up. The leadership team was aligned around the core principles of the design and it was built naturally and adjustments were made as we experienced our design in operation. Those core principles were:

- Start with the value adding process work and design roles that have broad accountability for all aspects of operation – safety, quality, service, cost and inventory. These are the operating technicians.
- Identify key support roles that are value added to the operating technicians and are attached to those operating units.
- Identify managing / coordinating roles that incorporate a broader cross functional view and are truly resources to their teams.
- Tie everything together with a series of processes that manage the operations continuously – by the hour, by the shift, by the day, by the week, by the month.

Although the entire leadership team bought in to the self-managing team concept, the capabilities of the leaders varied. Jim Harlow, our assembly manager, was the best at supporting this team approach and positioned himself in the best way to optimize the process. Phil Brown's reflections of Jim were; "He believed in the value of engaging his team, and that belief and his passion were contagious". In the highly technical areas (paint and injection), it was more difficult as the technicians had no interest in expanding into supervisory areas. It took the leader to be creative in order to get the best motivation level. On reflection, a key learning is; if you have a transition and leadership is not 100% committed to the approach, it will fail! We were fortunate to have the right leaders. The slightest change in personnel can take you back to ground zero!

At Measham we had 3 operating teams – Injection, Paint and Assembly. All direct and indirect resources were a part of those teams. A manager led and supported each team and reported to an overall Operations Manager. The Operations Manager reported to me as Plant Director – my direct reports included:

- Operations Manager
- Quality Manager
- Engineering Manager
- Logistics Manager
- HR Manager
- Finance Manager
- Operational Excellence Leader
- Jaguar Program Manager
- Rover Program Manager
- Administrative Assistant

In Automotive, a tier 1 supplier has two jobs – delivering the current production requirements and working continuously with the customer to secure the next generation models business. Since models change continuously, you have to ensure you are securing that business in the future. That is the plant's responsibility!! That is the role of the Program Managers at the plant – one dedicated to each customer.

Although the ramp-up tested the plants processes and systems, full ramp-up production was achieved in the designated timeframe. It's all about confidence and personal relationships. We knew we had a strong plant, and our relationships were very effective at working through issues. It was a great experience for me personally and professionally. To go to a different country and culture and lead the start-up of a plant from scratch was a once in a lifetime opportunity, and I was lucky to have been put in that position. Plastic Omnium saw value in me and took a chance, and I am grateful and deeply appreciative to them.

9. **MY DEPARTURE BUT THE PLANT CONTINUES TO IMPROVE**

At about the 1 ½ year mark of my time in the UK, I started to realize that, as a family, we needed to get back to the US. Although the kids were really enjoying the experience and starting to get settled, my wife was struggling with the rate of change and all the responsibility that she had to take on. The expatriate experience when you are with a large global company like Ford is not the same as with a much smaller company like Plastic Omnium. The larger companies paid relocation companies to support every aspect of the expatriate's needs. Plastic Omnium did not pay for relocation assistance, so Mary and I did everything in the transition. We didn't know how to secure long term housing agreements and ended up getting 6-month leases (that we thought automatically rolled over) and got evicted 3 times in 2 years. The pressure on my wife was tremendous as she worked to keep the kid's environment stable as we moved multiple times. Besides, the timing was right to get out oldest into his final 2 years of high school and prepared for college in the US.

At the 2-year mark, PO arranged for me to take on another role in the company that was based out of Rochester Hills, Michigan. It was as the overall project manager for a new plant starting up in Saltillo, MX that supported GM. GM was managing the project from their headquarters in Detroit and there were significant issues to work through.

The timing was good for me and the family and they needed a leadership presence as quickly as possible.

I kept the Measham team abreast of my plans so that when the time came for my departure, it was a seamless transition. I had dedicated 2 years of my life to building and supporting the team, and they were a strong unit that was not dependent on me anymore. I said my goodbyes and we had some final celebrations and I was off to the new role.

10. **LEARNING APPLIED TO SALTILLO**

As I took on the new role, the Measham experience was fresh in my mind and I was able to apply the learning immediately to the situation. The customer (GM) felt a disconnection with PO – they weren't getting the information that they asked for and, because of this, they were not confident that PO would deliver on their commitment. It was culturally a very complex situation: GM was the customer and requirements came from Detroit; the technology development and equipment design came from PO based in Lyon, France; and the plant operation and leadership were in Saltillo, MX. Every meeting involved 3 languages and many potential pitfalls. My role was simple – to give the customer confidence that we had a good plan with high probability of success, and to ensure that plans were in place to deliver that project on time. As I realized later, the best person to handle a role like this would be based out of Saltillo and speak all three languages. I did my best and we did get over the hump and got the plant into operation, the key learnings applied from Measham were:

- The customer is #1 and your interfaces must be seamless at all levels – program management and the operations.
- The program team has to operate as one unit with all functions out for the best interests of the customer and company.
- The plan must have alignment with the customer and all key functions within PO and must have sufficient contingency to allow for unplanned occurrences.

11. **THE RESULTS AND TRAJECTORY – STEP CHANGE AND THE PURSUIT OF PERFECTION**

As I left Measham, we were tracking towards achieving all of the objectives of the project and operation. We were most of the way up the learning curve, but still had some way to go to get to our stable operating standards. As I was immersed in crisis with the Saltillo start-up, I lost touch with the Measham progress. I thought about the team often, but never really reached out in a way to understand how they were progressing. I moved on with my career and had multiple stops after my UK experience. In 2007 (almost 10 years after the Measham experience), I was part of a due diligence team that was looking at an acquisition near Manchester in the UK about 1 ½ hours from Measham. I convinced my partner to come a little early with me to the UK and we would visit my old plant!! Dave Scrivens, my original partner in the beginning, was there to meet us and we took a tour of the plant. I was able to see some of the old crew and commented on how great the plant looked and how well they had done. And one guy said, "When you get it right from the beginning, it makes all the difference in the world!" My heart jumped a beat — I had put everything I had into the start-up and the people — and they were doing great. We did do it right from the beginning. We had a great mixture of cultures and diversity of people with everyone out for one end. PO in Measham had become a model for people to visit and learn from our experiences.

Steve Grainger reminded me recently "we must have done something right as we have had 6 extensions to the plant, we have 16 presses (compared to 5 at start-up), 2 paint lines (1 at start-up), and a robot bonding assembly line (none at start-up); and we are still here going strong!!" Dave Scrivens is currently working on a 7.5-million-pound expansion for the plant. Both Steve and Dave have been with Plastic Omnium for most of their careers.

12. **WRAP-UP**

Compared to my first case study, the circumstances were much different. Simpsonville was a turnaround — taking what existed and was operating and designing something better while gaining alignment throughout the organization. Measham was new with everything designed at the beginning as we were searching for the right players to engage in the process. Because Measham had the right players from the start, the alignment happened immediately at the interview process and the organizational design was worked continually and improved. It was a more common-sense design unlike Simpsonville where we used many models and concepts to guide our thinking and shift the culture. At Measham we had the right culture at the beginning.

For me, personally, there were big differences. At Simpsonville, I was in my own culture with the backing and active support of leaders who knew about what I was doing. In Measham, I was more on my own. Even though I had support if I needed it, it was more as requested!! I also had to deal with the French / English undertones in Measham which could be difficult to navigate at times. I was given more rope and the navigation was challenging. If I hadn't gone through Simpsonville, the Measham challenge would have been much more difficult. It required significant personal agility and a relentless drive to work through problems and with my team.

I was blessed to have the group of folks that I had. My only redo would have been to work as hard on the external relationships as I did with my internal team from the very beginning.

13. **CLOSING COMMENTS**

The PO experience allowed me to grow along a number of dimension: 1/ As a manufacturing leader and change agent, 2/ From a cross-cultural perspective, 3/ From a personal agility and drive perspective, and 4/ Supporting my family with all the challenges relative to settling in a different country. From a family perspective, every time we had a vacation or holiday, we were experiencing the culture in the UK and Europe. I am thankful and grateful to PO senior leaders for having confidence in me and providing me with opportunities to grow and make a contribution to the company. Looking back and considering my progress from Simpsonville to Measham, I can see how each experience informed and enabled the next one. That's the way that you would like your career to progress.

The 3rd case starts 14 years after my return from the UK. Again, much had transpired in the interim. I had taken on a lot of different roles. Each with their unique set of challenges, but none as significant as the first two cases. I was ready when this new opportunity presented itself.

PROJECT MADRID (2013-2017):
2 plants to 1 -- consolidation in Fem Care

CHAPTERS

1. Background and situation
2. The due diligence visit
3. Acquisition and relationship building
4. Cost focus and scoping out Project Madrid
5. Project approval and closure announcement
6. Initiating the project
7. The inventory build
8. Building the foundation and organization in Dover
9. Maintaining production and stability in Montreal during drawdown
10. The engineering project
11. The final stages
12. Project completion and the changing business landscape
13. Wrap-up
14. Closing comments

1. **BACKGROUND AND SITUATION**

I was the Operations Director for the Global Fem Care business in 2013. I had been in that role since early 2010. Our business provided a portion of the offerings in the Fem Pro category in the market. We produced about 1.3 billion tampons of Sport and Gentle Glide annually. I joined Playtex in 2006 as an Operations Director in Ohio responsible for Wet Ones wipes and Diaper Genie, and then took on a Lean leadership role prior to moving into Fem Care. Playtex was acquired by Energizer in 2008, and the Fem Care brand became a part of their Personal Care portfolio of businesses. (which included Schick, Banana Boat, Hawaiian Tropic, Wet Ones, Diaper Genie, Sport & Gentle Glide Tampons and Playtex Infant Care products)

Playtex was in the #2 position in tampons in the US market in 2013. It was the innovator of the plastic applicator tampon which eventually dominated the market and put Playtex as the #1 supplier in that category. With P&G's introduction of their brand in the early 2000s, the dynamics shifted, and they became the #1 supplier. Their spending to support the category was much higher than Playtex, and the gap continued to grow in the succeeding years. The impact on Playtex was significant as volume declined from a high of 2.3 billion tampons to 1.3 billion in 2013 causing the plant to be underutilized and putting significant pressure on costs. Due to the nature of the business being in a highly regulated environment, the required fixed costs necessary to compete in this market were high.

Part of the job of the operations team was to support the brand requirements while continually looking for opportunities to reduce costs ahead of the volume declines. One area of activity was looking for ways to better utilize the manufacturing facility. This included looking at other businesses that might fit into the plant footprint and cover some of the fixed costs. We had investigated a contract manufacturing situation with J&J in the past, as well as, other similar types of opportunities.

Johnson and Johnson's situation in their Fem Pro business in North America was similar to ours but with different circumstances. Their North American business was in decline, with most of their sales and growth in the rest of the world. The Montreal Plant was union and in a high cost environment while the exchange rate was moving towards parity with the dollar. Part of the original rationale on locating the plant in Montreal was the exchange rate advantages and having a world class facility in North America to support a growing business in that market. Over the years J&J increased the priority of their drug portfolio which offered much higher returns. With this move, the Fem Pro business, in particular in North America, received reduced investments. In 2013, J&J leadership was actively looking for buyers for that business. The position of EPC (Energizer Personal Care) operations leadership was that this would be a great opportunity to gain synergies and better manage the high fixed cost position. Word came down that "we were in the game"!

2. **THE DUE DILIGENCE VISIT**

After spending 3 years leading an operation that was continually losing volume and adjusting costs to support changing realities, the thought of acquiring the J&J North American Fem Pro business and the Montreal plant was exciting! I knew it could be a game changer for us with best practices learning and leveraging the synergies that existed between the two plants. I was fortunate to be included in the due diligence visit planned in April of 2013 to the Montreal plant. Our cover for the visit was as a consultant team touring the plant and meeting with leadership on logistic opportunities. It was a small team including: my boss Chris Crowell (VP of EPC Global Operations), Ricardo De Oliveira (Director of R&D for the Fem Care business), some other acquisition specialists and myself. The visit included a tour of the site and operations, and a presentation on the history of the business and site and information relative to the key sales and cost factors that drive the financials. Sylvain Maher (the Plant Manager) did most of the presenting and our first impression was very good.

As I was listening intently to all the presentations, some key points struck me:

- It was a union plant with a very high wage rate compared to Dover and no ability to use temporary workers for low skilled work.
- The total number of salary and wage colleagues in the plant were much higher compared to Dover.
- The benefits cost and loading was almost twice the US rate.

- The direction of the exchange rate trend over the previous 10 years was moving toward parity with the US dollar.

I took notes and that night in the hotel room did a high-level spreadsheet on the impact of moving everything to Dover to fill out the footprint. The assumptions included capital, synergies from consolidation, savings from wage rates and benefit differences, and a general timing of the consolidation process. The results of my top line assessment was that a plant consolidation would have a tremendous impact on the cost position of the business. (It would turn out to be very close to the final numbers on the capital appropriation request a year later). I reviewed my thinking with the team at breakfast the next day, and we filed the information for future use. Key questions like technical complexity and would our footprint in Dover support a consolidation were left unanswered at that point. I left the Montreal plant excited about the possibilities knowing that there was much work to be done to complete the analysis.

In follow-up meetings to the visit, we continued to refine our numbers for operations synergies from the acquisition. Our assumptions ended up being much more conservative and did not include the full plant consolidation but being able to leverage 2 more cost effective sites in support of the North American business. There were also logistical savings through better access to US markets for J&J product. We provided the operations synergies feedback to the acquisition team and awaited word. We didn't hear anything for a month and were beginning to think that we didn't get the business. It turns out J&J was pursuing another opportunity that didn't pan out – and after a couple of month delay, we found out in July of 2013 that we got the business!! It would take to the end of October to close the deal, in the meantime, a project was initiated to support the integration of the J&J North American Fem Pro business and the Montreal plant into EPC. I would be the operations lead on that team.

3. ACQUISITION AND RELATIONSHIP BUILDING

With the close of the acquisition phase of the project at the end of October in 2013, we planned a celebration event at the Montreal plant immediately after it became final. It would be a big deal for Energizer as even the Bunny would be there to participate. I worked with Sylvain (the plant manager) and the company communications director to plan the event. Sylvain was the main orchestrator and the 2-day event included meetings with the plant leadership team, union leadership team, all shifts and 1 to 1 meetings with the key senior leaders at the plant. The event was attended by all the key operations leaders in EPC and the President of the Energizer Canadian business. Sylvain continued to demonstrate a strong leadership presence and it was clear to see that he was highly respected within the plant. This was our top leadership's first exposure to him and they came away from the visit knowing that our new plant was in good hands.

Part of the agenda for this initial visit was an overview of the business and the plant operation. Sylvain and some others provided the background information and we got a first up-close look at the cost factors and structure of the plant. You could see from the safety and quality performance of the plant that it was top notch and you could also see the impact of the drop off in production volumes over the years as J&J reduced their investments in those markets. We set an expectation during this first visit of a short and long-term cost reduction plan. We shared with Sylvain and his team Playtex' OP10 Program and asked that the Montreal plant develop their own plan in line with it. OP10 was defined as a focus to improve operating profit for the business by 10% in 3 years. It was framed as not just a cost reduction program but a business improvement one. The focus was equally cost reduction and revenue generation. Sylvain and his team were very open to the idea and had already implemented many cost reductions as volume dropped off over the years – we were asking for more aggressive reductions.

My boss had developed a strong bond with Sylvain since the due diligence visit. After the acquisition was announced in July he visited the plant for a general communication with the Canadian HR director Krystine Jankowski. Both became the faces of Energizer to the Montreal team. Chris and I had conversations about merging the Montreal operation under my area of responsibility to be able to provide more direct support to Sylvain and his team, but we knew the communication of that change to Sylvain had to be made in the right way. Chris talked to Sylvain about him reporting to me because, as Chris said, "Buff has access to all the resources and relationships that you and your team need to be successful", and with that Sylvain and I started to develop our relationship. I was always conscious of the importance of Chris never losing touch with the plant as his relationship to the plant was still a very important one. From that point forward Sylvain and I would build a strong personal and professional bond.

One of the benefits of having a senior Energizer leader at an event like this one was the possibility of hitching a ride back home on the corporate jet!! What a deal, we left the Montreal plant and went directly to the corporate jet at the airport and left. We dropped Dave VerNooy (our most senior operations leader) in Connecticut and then landed at Dover Air Force Base – now that's what I'm talking about!

4. **COST FOCUS AND SCOPING OUT PROJECT MADRID**

While Montreal was working on their version of OP10, the Energizer corporate wide cost reduction program (Project Transformers) was in high gear. No stone was left unturned in the search for cost reduction opportunities. A benchmarking study comparing Energizer to their key competitors showed a major gap. We knew during the due diligence visit that a plant consolidation was one possibility but in the new Transformer's environment it became a probability. We started our planning even before the acquisition was closed and were comparing options which boiled down to: 1/ two very skinny plants – one Internal Sanitary Protection (ISP – tampons in Dover) & one External Sanitary Protection (ESP – pads/liner in Montreal); and 2/ Complete consolidation in one plant (Dover or Montreal). Multiple high-level analysis were completed over a 3-month period. The choice would be between 2 skinny plants and total consolidation in Dover with shutdown of the Montreal plant. The detailed financials would be based on these scenarios – we would do the work but A.T. Kearney (the Project Transformers consultants) would be involved at every turn.

I visited the Montreal plant before the end of 2013 or about 1 ½ months after the acquisition celebration. Sylvain and his team had completed the initial scoping of their OP10 program and had already defined programs to meet the requirements. It was clear that their team was very strong, and I thoroughly enjoyed working with them. At that time, the work on plant consolidation was confidential with only a small group involved. It was important to me to get back to Montreal before the holidays, to ensure my connection with Sylvain and his team was robust. I also initiated a weekly call with Sylvain to stay in tough and be able to provide proactive support. Those calls would be "top priority" for both Sylvain and I as we were both committed to building a strong relationship.

In early January of 2014, the Fem Care plant consolidation project was named Project Madrid (the name was carried over from the J&J acquisition project which was the same) and moved to a detailed planning phase. At this point I felt it was necessary to bring Sylvain and his HR Manager (Irene Mascolo) in the loop on the planning. I was fortunate that both Chris and Dave VerNooy (Chris' boss) knew the importance of trust in any relationship and supported my decision to involve them. I traveled back to Montreal in late January to give both Sylvain and Irene a brief on the situation and ask for their support. At that time there were still the 2 scenarios in play for Montreal – either a complete shutdown or a much smaller plant with just pads/liners production. It was quite a shock for both of them especially after the celebration just a couple of months earlier. Although they both knew that any acquisition came with the need for cost savings, they were hoping that Energizer would be growing the business with additional volumes for the Montreal plant. They were both very professional and I could see how fortunate we were to have them in critical positions.

From January to June Sylvain and I worked to get Montreal fully integrated into the EPC organization and process. We established all the right connections for he and his team and ensured that the changeover from J&J systems happened in the most effective way. One of the more challenging changes was moving from J&J distribution centers to Energizer ones. In order to do this cost effectively, the business dropped the inventory as low as possible before moving it and then ramped production volumes back up to get to target inventory levels. What we began to realize is that Montreal's planning group was very strong, just like Playtex. Sylvain and his team were off to a great start with EPC. Their OP10 was starting to take shape and savings were beginning to be realized. But he and I knew that there was big change on the horizon.

5. **PROJECT APPROVAL AND CLOSURE ANNOUNCEMENT**

After many iterations the decision was made to recommend full consolidation in Dover and the closure of the Montreal plant. A CAR (Capital Authorization Request) was developed for Project Madrid. It was just one of a number of major consolidations and cost reduction projects for EPC operations. After careful review of all the projects and CARs, it was decided to move forward with just Project Madrid based on the IRR (rate of return). We were very aggressive with the timeline for the project (3 years) as compared to the other shave consolidation projects which made the project more attractive. The project was submitted and received Energizer board level approval in Mid-June of 2014. We now had to plan the communication, at this point only a small working group was aware of the project.

The primary players in the development and implementation of the communication strategy and plan were Canadian HR and operational leadership (Krystine and Sylvain) and EPC operational leadership (Chris and myself). Irene (Montreal's HR Manager) had resigned and this added complexity to the process. Energizer legal and external consultants were engaged to ensure thorough vetting of the ideas and ultimately EPC leadership made the final decision. The choice of strategy boiled down to a "peel the onion" approach or only announce the immediate activity ahead to keep all options open in the future and, perhaps, to leave some hope for the Montreal folks. The other option was to announce the full closure and provide transparency throughout the communication process. We were fortunate to have local Montreal consultants who shared examples of plants who adopted the different strategies, and their recommendation was to be open from the beginning because trust was critical in projects of long duration where you have to maintain a quality operation for a significant period of time. The operational leaders intuitively understood this but HR and legal needed a lot of convincing to bring them on board. We made our recommendation of the communication strategy and plan to higher level and they approved it. We were now down to the detail planning.

The announcement was set for July 8, 2014 in Montreal. All aspects of the communication, both internal and external, were planned at the detail level. Chris would take the lead in the communication on site in Montreal. The intention was that he was the company representative and the decision maker, while I was working with the plant and business to carry out the decision that had been made. Chris didn't want me to play any role – he wanted to give me cover to enable me to carry out my role effectively in the future. For the day of the announcement, there would only be 4 company representatives that were external to the plant – Chris, Krystine (Canadian HR), Ricardo (Director of Fem Care R&D) and me. The process was similar to the acquisition celebration just 9 months earlier. Meetings would be with the plant leadership team, union leadership team, shift teams and 1 to 1's with the key leaders at the plant. These meetings would be extremely difficult given the topic, but we would be prepared with open communication on the situation and the plan and would outline the things that we would do to support all the colleagues in Montreal. In the 1 to 1 meetings with the Montreal senior leaders I listened and responded to their concerns. I also asked them to consider coming to Dover to help with the relocation of the new equipment. Most were not interested but one guy, Jean-Pierre Tougas (JP as he became universally known), said he would like to come. He would become a key player in Madrid's success.

As the communication was happening in Montreal, it was being made via announcement throughout Energizer and to the public. It was viewed with mixed emotions – for the Montreal community it was sadness, for the Dover community it with a sense of opportunity, the rest of Energizer felt for the Montreal colleagues but knew it was an important business decision, and for the business community it was a positive for Energizer with the expectation of improved profitability. For me, it was mixed as well. I was beginning to develop a strong bond with the Montreal plant – the plant had a proud history and now that was ending – it was sad. But I was looking forward to the project. It was large in scope and very complex and would be a good way to wind down my career. From a challenge point of view, I couldn't have had a better situation but there was much work to do.

6. **INITIATING THE PROJECT**

With the communication process complete we could now work openly on the project. We had started the inventory build prior to the announcement and had asked Sylvain to make that happen but in a way that didn't raise any questions. We knew that we would be pressed to deliver the project in the 3-year timeframe and the inventory build was key to that. We had a defined project management process and used it to start to fill out the team. We were assigned a program manager from Milford, CT (EPC operations HQ). All major new product and cost reduction projects are run by program managers to ensure professionalism and continuity. Our program manager was Dale Neely. Dale was a very experienced shave guy who had diverse experience and had been in automotive earlier in his career. We were fortunate to have him – he was a driver and collaborator. Dale had all the skills that a good program manager needed but was unique in his ability to sense problem areas and lean into them relentlessly to ensure they were being addressed in the most effective way. He would become my partner for the duration of the project.

The project team was made up of all the senior leaders of the functions that were directly involved and impacted by the change. They included operations, R&D, quality, engineering, HR – both Montreal and Dover would have their counterparts on the team. Dale and I decided that we would have bi-monthly planning and update meetings in Montreal to start with. We felt that face to face interaction was critical at this early stage to build the teamwork necessary for the project's success. This also enabled the Montreal plant to fully engage others in the project and gave the Dover team exposure to everything in Montreal. We also had bi-monthly updates with the EPC operations senior leadership. This was critical to ensure alignment on the direction and highlight issues that would require their support. These meetings were timed after the project team meetings to provide the most updated information. We initiated this process immediately and had our first meeting in September – 2 months after the announcement.

We held to this routine and, looking back, it was a key reason for the success of the project. This project brought together 3 different cultures: Schick culture in Milford, CT; the Playtex culture in Dover, DE; and the Montreal culture. The dynamics of the interactions would play out over the 3 years and our strong routine was able to align us on a continual basis. The Schick culture reflected the northeast way of doing things – direct, identifying issues head-on and action oriented. The Playtex culture reflected more of a southern way of doing things – indirect where social interaction was important in allowing people to discuss things thoroughly. In Montreal, although most of the senior leaders spoke good English, it was their 2nd language and ensuring understanding was important. They also had been part of the J&J culture for years and as such were conservative and very functionally oriented. Our project management process allowed us to navigate this landscape effectively. Towards the end of the project, Dave VerNooy, the senior operations leader in the company made a surprise visit to one of our leadership meetings in Montreal. As we were walking to dinner on a beautiful night in Old Town, he said to me: "Buff, I'm amazed at the quality of interaction today at the meeting, everyone listening and focused on doing things in the best interest of the project, even as the Montreal people are facing a very difficult situation." That was the tone that we set from day 1.

7. **THE INVENTORY BUILD**

Shortly after announcing the project and the closure of the Montreal plant, it came to my attention that Nick Spadavecchia might be available to come join us in Fem Care. I knew Nick well and had worked with him on a number of occasions. I knew him to be an expert in his field and a relentless, driven guy around getting results. I felt we needed someone like him to orchestrate the product and material planning of the project. After discussion with Nick and others, I was able to make it happen. Having Nick on our team was one of the keys to the success of the project.

Nick immediately took charge of the planning for the inventory build. Both planning teams, Montreal and Dover, reported to him and he quickly established strong working relationships with the groups. The inventory build process was very complex and a function of many variables – Montreal production rates, Dover learning curve and production rates, time to shutdown/move/start-up the equipment, demand level and variability. This was the world that Nick knew best, and his team managed this project in an excellent manner. The level of capability in both Montreal and Dover planning groups was very high. They were all drivers and had high expectation for their respective operations teams. They had the unique ability to "crack the whip" yet were consummate team players. Ultimately, the inventory build had to cover anywhere from 4 to 6 months of production outage time due to the work of disconnecting, moving and reconnecting the equipment; and the learning curve in Dover. We had the best of the best in Nick's department running the show, and we knew that with each move of a line we would get continually better at the entire process due to experience.

It was amazing to me how effectively this process was managed. Even during the highly uncertain process towards the end of Montreal's operation, we never suffered a product outage of any significant duration except in OB tampons. OB was a different story and one of the first processes to move and our learning curve was far off planned levels due to a number of factors. It was old equipment and more of an art to operate. We had identified a couple of Montreal experts to come to Dover to help in the start-up, but they left the company early and were not available. Also, the union colleagues in that part of the plant would not work in the presence of our operators and mechanics. This was just a bad situation overall with everything going the wrong direction. We eventually got resources in and recovered but it took of 6 months to get caught up.

Another aspect that Nick managed seamlessly was the organizational evolution – from a 2-plant organization with most of the activity planned out of Montreal to a 1 plant organization planned and managed out of Dover. He orchestrated the drawdown in Montreal and ramp-up in Dover over the 3-year timeframe in a way that was supportive of all Montreal colleagues and extended the capability of the already high performing Dover team.

8. BUILDING THE FOUNDATION AND ORGANIZATION IN DOVER

The initial planning for the project had the addition of colleagues in Dover at 272. The plant was operating at around 450. This represented a significant addition to the plant and overall, to the state of Delaware. It was a significant project. Over the 3-year duration of the project we had 3 primary missions: 1/ To continue to operate both plants in a way that met all requirements – safety, quality, delivery, cost and inventory; 2/ To meet all brand requirements from each plant to include new products and commercial innovation; and 3/ To execute Project Madrid to the cost and timing requirements of the CAR (Capital Appropriation Request). We had about a year before the first processes were moved and needed to have a fully trained organization on the receiving end. One of the first decisions early on was to search for an experienced future leader for Fem Care that would take my place when we were a single plant operation and, would lead Dover from its current state to the new organizational level. Bill Bunn joined the organization just after the announcement in August of 2014. He was a very experienced guy who I had crossed paths with on a number of occasions. He had been an Engineering Director with Kimberly Clark and had led multiple manufacturing organizations after that. He was "what the doctor ordered" and we were fortunate to have him. This allowed me to move Tom Spiezio full time to the project. Tom was the operations leader for the project and was responsible for ensuring that the knowledge transfer happened such that we were successful in Dover. He also was to interact with HR to assure qualified colleagues were in place in Dover to meet the production requirements at start-up.

Tom was a long time Playtex leader who had done everything over his career. He had a high EI (emotional intelligence) and had great relationships with the shop floor colleagues. He was an on the floor leader who always led from the front. In this role, he would have to do everything to ensure the knowledge transfer happened effectively. That included things like: recruiting operators and mechanics to live and train in Montreal over extended periods of time, making arrangement for all travel and accommodations in Montreal, do the same for Montreal colleagues coming to Dover, working with training personnel to get the knowledge transferred from a French platform to English, ensure the receiving organization in Dover was ready to start-up the new processes, and many other small and large activities. Tom would be the link between Bill and Sylvain and was instrumental in the success of the start-up.

JP Tougas had formally accepted our offer and agreed to come to Dover to live and work. He became the ESP (External Sanitary Protection – Pads and Liners) leader in Dover, even while he was still actively leading the Montreal operation. Sylvain, Bill, Tom and JP became the core of Project Madrid's operational leadership. They ensured that resources were available in Dover as needed to support the start-up. JP and Sylvain knew all the players in Montreal and would relentlessly recruit them for "Dover Duty"!! We were fortunate to have such high-quality leaders driven for the success of the project.

The HR teams in Montreal and Dover faced daunting tasks. The drawdown of the plant in Montreal and the ramp-up in Dover presented different challenges but we were fortunate to have solid leaders making it happen every day. Early on it became clear that getting highly skilled folks in the electrical and some engineering areas would be challenging, but HR adjusted the process to open things up and we were able to get back on track. They would schedule stand-alone job fairs throughout the state in sufficient number to get us the folks that we needed. No one in the state was hiring at the level or pace that we were, yet our HR team in Dover got us where we needed to be. The HR contribution to this project was enormous and I was grateful to have had great support at both plants.

The organizational design for the new plant operation was completed and aligned to by the leadership team. The Montreal approach of business units (BU) was adopted in Dover, so there would be 2 business units in the plant – ESP (External Sanitary Protection – Stayfree pads and Carefree liners) and ISP (Internal Sanitary Protection – Sport, Gentle Glide and OB tampons). Each BU would have all the support resources necessary within their group including maintenance and engineering. There would be a small centralized engineering and maintenance group outside of the BUs. We went with the model of decentralization to ensure resources were focused on the value adding processes. We had a lot of discussion around how much out of the BU? We decided to err on the side of more in than out.

In our project plan we timed the addition of resources to allow for training and learning curve time. Because we were not a large company with lots of money, staffing additions were just in time. By doing this we added risk to the project, as we ended up having recruiting problems early on. The project just didn't have the money to significantly front end load the process. Looking back, we should have done more front-end loading of the organization, because the price we paid far outweighed what cost we would have incurred. We ended up having to react to the shortage of personnel and skills with contract and temporary colleagues at a cost premium to the project. This was a key learning for our team.

When we designed the ESP organization, we created operating technicians with an expectation of a high level of capability and self-management. The recruiting and selection process was rigorous, and we ended up with a very strong team. We tried to build the capabilities and accountabilities at the operator and team level to drive better response time and decision making. The contrast with our legacy tampon operations was stark. Even though we had upgraded the expectations and skill level, the actual operation was very old school with a high dependency on maintenance and engineers for support. But with the amount of change in the plant, we didn't have the time or resources to drive organizational improvement in that area – it would have to wait until after the project was complete.

It's important to note that the Montreal support to the project was far beyond what was expected. Initially we didn't think that we would get a lot of volunteers to come to Dover. But all it took was a couple of Montreal guys to come and then go back to Montreal and say: "those guys in Dover are pretty good and they really take care of you"!! That along with JP, Tom's and Sylvain's relentless recruiting helped save the day for us!! If not for Montreal's support, we would have been in a tough spot.

I began to realize early on in the organization design that my position would be eliminated. I knew it was the right thing to do, and I felt that I would have options at the end of the project – one option would be retirement as I would be closing in on 65 at the time of the last machine start-up. I had a lot of trust that the organization would do the right thing by me, so I had no concerns. But looking back on it, I'm amazed at how easily I eliminated my job!! Wow, there's a learning in that!!

9. **MAINTAINING PRODUCTION AND STABILITY IN MONTREAL DURING DRAWDOWN**

In the first 2-3 months following the announcement of closure we had a massive wave of resignations that created problems in the operation of the facility. Sylvain and his new HR manager (Valerie Gagnon) had to quickly engage in a hiring process just to enable the plant to meet the production requirements. This was a wake-up call for the Montreal leadership team to put in place a strong retention plan. The team responded as the situation stabilized after that initial period.

Our initial long-term assumptions relative to Montreal's performance in terms of the inventory build were deterioration over time. The thinking was that as Montreal lost people to other jobs in the community, their expertise and general competence would go down and this would affect performance. Our belief was that the closer to the end date, the lower the morale and that would affect performance as well. We were also concerned with the risk to safety and quality based on the factors above. We had a lot of discussion about possible sabotage on the equipment and how it could adversely impact our start-up in Dover. We discussed having a strong salary and guard presence during the key stages of equipment breakdown and preparation for shipment. But, at the end of the day, the importance of trust won out. None of these concerns played out for the duration of the project. We did feel on occasion that there might have been sabotage — but the number of cases was small. The actual performance was exceptional the entire time which included:

- World class safety and quality performance.
- Major source of Fem Care savings from 2013 baseline.
- Excellent service.
- Much improved inventory control from J&J historical.

Sylvain and his team were very creative with their organizational planning. When a salary colleague left, they looked for opportunities to combine roles and allow others to significantly increase their capabilities and compensation. When the timing came for a drawdown of both salary and wage colleagues, they allowed people to volunteer as long as the plant performance was not put at risk. These and other changes in policy allowed people to have flexibility and options to consider. It also created a very positive environment up until the last day the plant was open. Sylvain was also open and very proactive in working with the union. He listened intently to their concerns and worked with them and his leadership team to find solutions. The Dover and Montreal relationship was as sister plants — each willing to do whatever was necessary to help a situation. Bill and Sylvain provided that type of leadership within their plants.

Up to the end, that flexibility was maintained. Sylvain had a great opportunity that surfaced, and the plant was covered through other leadership options in the final months. We approved his released in order to allow him to get his severance. I had to step up and support the remaining plant leadership group, but that was how we operated to the end. We were one team looking out for one another.

10. **THE ENGINEERING PROJECT**

The engineering portion of Project Madrid involved creating the infrastructure in Dover to receive and operate the manufacturing equipment, move the equipment from Montreal to Dover and validate the initial production. In the Fem Care world of Class 1 and 2 medical devices, validation is a big thing. It means proving through data that the product and process are capable of meeting specifications at the prescribed production rates. That is the point that engineering hands over the manufacturing equipment and process to operations.

The scope of the project included:

- Relocating 15 OB automats (tampon processing)
- Relocating 3 OB packaging lines
- Relocating all OB supporting fiber opening and blending equipment (tampon pre-processing)
- Relocating 6 Stayfree production lines
- Relocating 6 Carefree production lines
- Expand the plant footprint by 40,000 SF
- Upgrade building throughout the new production areas to meet FDA environmental standards.

Wayne Rossi was the leader of all engineering aspects of the project. He was a long time Playtex guy who lived for these types of projects. He was a big picture guy whose strength was to frame large projects and build the organization necessary to execute them. He knew who could do what, when to go outside to get a contractor, and which were the best contractors. A lifetime of experience had put him in the position to be our engineering go to guy. He knew that we could handle the site infrastructure aspect of the project and get it done on time. Montreal had introduced Berman (who had done much of the infrastructure work in Montreal) to Wayne and their contribution to the site preparation would be crucial to the success of the project. But in the relocation of the lines, many of which were state of the art, high speed electronic technology, he didn't feel we had the capability to handle it and should look for someone who had "been there, done that"!! We got ahold of one contractor, interviewed him and started to use him early on for the relocation project. Then, Rick Burrow dropped in on us!! What a find — Wayne Rossi had earned his salary for the duration of the project!! Rick was an ex J&J engineering leader who literally had "been there and done that"!!! Rick knew what to do and how to do it, and from the beginning was our leader for that aspect of the project. Wayne listened to Rick and provided whatever support was needed. Rick told us that we would get better with each line, and once he mobilized his team that is what happened.

Managing the validation aspect of the project was the main source of tension within the organization. The engineers were driven to get the project done, while the quality folks wanted to ensure the validation was done correctly with no defects. No defects was a tall order with the scope and scale of the equipment we were validating. Early on we had major issues between the functions, it got better over time and the last validations were pretty impressive. At the end of the day, everyone was out for the best interests of the project and gave a little – always keeping their eye on the ball!

In the last year of the project, the engineering aspect went like clock-work, as least from my perspective. But if you ask Wayne, he would say everyday was a challenge – to do a quality job and stay on track with necessary timing. Because he led that way -- focusing each day on the requirements for that day -- and using weekends as surge capacity, a very complex project became manageable. When I would take my walks around the project, I never ceased to be amazed. Watching a Carefree liners production line run 3200 pieces / minute consistently is so impressive. Unless you are really focusing and concentrating, you can't actually see the product flow because it's so fast!! The engineering team under Rick and Wayne's leadership was very strong and they did an outstanding job. Thinking back, we were fortunate to have such a high-quality group.

11. **THE FINAL STAGES**

We entered early 2017 with good momentum and tracking towards an August completion date for the project. That is the time that the last production line is validated and in operation. This represented a 2-month delay from the original timing outlined in the CAR. The CAR had been developed in June of 2014 confidentially in a small group without vetting from many of the most knowledgeable folks. In my mind, we had done the job as promised. It would take until March of 2018 to complete the validation of all products as each of the lines had to cycle through its particular range of products once it was operating.

If we look at the duration of the project, you can see the learning and growth that the entire organization experienced. OB was the first large department to move. We were still getting our feet wet and it was extremely challenging. We fell behind, put ourselves in a hole, and relentlessly dug out and recovered. There were many learnings that were incorporated in future moves. However, OB was unique as I mentioned earlier. It was very old equipment dependent on the specific knowledge of the operator and mechanic. When we decided to move the department all at once and lost access to much of Montreal's knowledge, it was a recipe for disaster. We were starting up all the lines at the same time and couldn't handle the frequency of problems nor solve them quickly. Another strategy would have been multiple moves to enable us to learn more effectively and have a situation that was more manageable, but this would have extended the timing which was a key metric for success.

The pads and liners equipment was much different. They were newer equipment that were continuous flow and had updated technology. The range of the ages was from 20-year old technology to 5-year old. We had a much more manageable flow of equipment from Montreal to Dover and had better engineering and maintenance resource availability for these moves. That was the learning – twofold – spread the flow of equipment from Montreal to a manageable level and secure more resources to support the assembly and start-up work in Dover. The pads and liners part of the project continued to get better with each line move. The final lines seemed to fly together as teams coordinated closely at each stage of the project. But as Rick Burrow would say to me over and over again – "it's all about the knowledge transfer and being able to operate the lines consistently every day."!!

We projected that it would take a couple of years after the Montreal plant closure to sell the facility. Our financials had included a significant carrying cost during that period. Sylvain worked closely with our Edgewell contact to tour prospective buyers around the facility and answer questions. As luck would have it, we found a buyer and were able to sell the facility shortly after the close of the plant. There was just enough time to clean it up before the new owner took possession. Wow, it was a perfect scenario. The price wasn't what we had hoped for – but it was a good price and we would have no carrying costs.

As the plant in Montreal was winding down in its last month of operation, I made a couple of trips to support the team and stay connected to the process. Sylvain had moved on to another job, and I wanted to be there for the team in the final stages. We would have dinners out and it was an opportunity to express our appreciation to that team. The key external leaders who consistently engaged directly with the Montreal team were Ricardo De Oliveira (Director of R&D), Krystine Jankowski (Director of HR), and Nick Spadavecchia (Fem Value Stream Manager). I appreciated their continuous involvement in the project and the plant throughout the process.

12. **PROJECT COMPLETION AND BUSINESS ENVIRONMENT**

With the start-up of the last production line in August of 2017, a reflection on the results would show:

- OB learning curve was long and continues to be a challenge to reach and sustain Montreal performance level.
- Pads and liners is mixed with most of the newer technology at learning curve level while the older technology is more challenging.
- The project capital cost was managed to the CAR level (after a supplemental funding request was approved early on in the project).
- The overall savings for the project are less based on significant reduction in production volume from CAR level, and the project extension due to longer learning curves.

The business environment in Fem Care has shifted significantly from the beginning of the project. With the J&J acquisition, low single digit volume growth was projected. In reality, significant declines have been experienced and placed pressure on costs at a time when the new operations are still in their early stages of development. This has impacted the stability of the Dover manufacturing environment as it seeks to find the right organizational make-up and size to support the future business. With the pressure on inventory management equal to cost, there are more frequent changeovers which also impact costs and productivity.

With the financials for the project off the mark, the questions most frequently asked are: "Was the project successful?" "Should we have done it?" "Will it enable us to be more effective in the future?" My response would be: We completed an extremely complex project in the timeframe that was originally planned and significantly improved the cost position of the business. With the current decline in sales in a regulated industry that drives high infrastructure and fixed costs, the plant consolidation effort was necessary. If we hadn't made the move, we would now be in a much higher cost position than pre-move. The last 2 questions are clearly a strong YES. Much of the financial miss came from lower volumes and the impact of inventory adjustment necessitated during the final stages of the project due to significant drop-off in demand.

On reflection, key success factors and significant challenges include:

- Key success factors:
  1. Establish a collaborative process with broad engagement throughout and open communications where trust can flourish. (The Dover – Montreal linkage was seamless)
  2. Provide proactive support to the closing facility to enable them to meet their business requirements while drawing down the operation to the end. (Montreal had many challenges and they needed unconditional support)

3. Maximize training time and support in both plants to accelerate learning curve performance.
4. Plan validations using a cross functional team early on and remain closely connected until completion.
5. Maximize resource availability from validation through start-up to accelerate learning curve performance.

- Significant challenges to overcome included:
    1. Initial communication of closure and how to engage Montreal in the best way to move forward.
    2. Stabilization and maintenance of Montreal performance.
    3. Engineering project mobilization to meet timeline requirements – right resources needed immediately.
    4. Knowledge transfer in a union facility that is closing.
    5. Resource needs early in the project are much greater than the steady state situation.
    6. Maintaining a FDA Class 1 production site while in the midst of significant construction activity in the same plant.
    7. Increasing organizational size by over ½ in a way that evolves the culture in the direction that you want.

13. **WRAP-UP**

I retired at the end of September in 2017. At that point, we were at a single plant operation and the reins had been passed to the next generation (Actually, Bill Bunn is almost my age! – but that's another story!). The organization is starting to settle at the right level, but that is always dependent on the success of the business and the level of sales. The standards continue to improve at the plant as capability and competence grow. From the time of the due diligence to my retirement, it's been 4 ½ years. Fem Care operations is now in a better position to support the brand and business, but there are new challenges on the horizon. In the new Amazon led world, manufacturing to on-line demand will be one of the capabilities necessary to stay competitive. I'm confident in the organization and leadership and their ability to answer the call!!

14. **CLOSING COMMENTS**

I am blessed to be able to work with such a great group of folks in a project as rewarding as Madrid. I've mentioned the name of some of the key leaders as they came to mind naturally, but there are many more who were instrumental in the project's success. We had great leadership from the top at all levels. People ask me about Edgewell and I say, at the end of the day, they are good people that are very smart. Our top leadership was always challenging but supportive. They were relentless around issue resolution but didn't get in the way. I'd especially like to thank my two senior leaders:

- Chris Crowell (VP of Global Operations and my boss) for providing this leadership opportunity to me and supporting me every step of the way.
- Dave VerNooy (Senior VP of Global Technology and Operation and Chris' boss) for staying connected to me throughout the process and engaging me directly in areas of opportunity, and for his support.

OVERALL SUMMARY

While writing the different stories and reflecting on those respective time periods, I realized how each situation built on the previous one. In the Simpsonville case, I was a relatively new plant manager and relied on the guidance and support of a consultant and my boss. The frameworks used in that case were needed to help my team and I understand where we were headed and how to get there. The path was planned with a lot of structure and many systems were developed to guide our way.

In Measham, our team started small and grew to a complete plant organization. We all shared a vision coming in and worked every day to realize that vision. Although we used consultants on occasion, it was mainly for renewal processes to adjust course. My capability had grown significantly, and I was confident in my ability to lead the development of the new plant.

Project Madrid was the culmination of my career. It was a higher-level role where I needed to guide the project team and respective plant organizations toward a defined future state. It was about team alignment and effectively working through issues. Even though I was involved in the details at the project and organizational planning, I was more of a guide and supporter to the other senior leaders.

My career has evolved to the point where I am now in a position to help others. So, if you need help, give me a call!

ACKNOWLEDGEMENTS

After completion of the drafts for each case study, I reconnected with my respective teams during those time frames and send them a copy and asked for comments and suggestions. I had not been in contact with many of the folks for a long time. It was so great hearing from everyone and getting their take on the situations. I've incorporated their feedback in the final draft. I am grateful for them taking the time out of their busy lives to read, reflect and respond to me in such a positive way.

Writing a book about my experiences creates mixed feelings. To reflect and capture things in a way that others can benefit from is rewarding. But, it also involves others who lived it with me, and I get nervous as I throw my work out there for friends and the general public to view. I've tried to be honest in my narrative and reflection and stay positive as I wrote about the more negative situations in my career. I hope it will be useful to others in their work, careers and life.